EPIPHANY

Interpreting the Lessons of the Church Year

Mark Allan Powell

EPIPHANY

PROCLAMATION 6 | SERIES B

FORTRESS PRESS | MINNEAPOLIS

PROCLAMATION 6
Interpreting the Lessons of the Church Year
Series B, Epiphany

Scripture quotations, unless otherwise indicated, are from the New Revised Standard Version
Bible, copyright © 1989 by the Division of Christian Education of the National Council of
Churches in the U.S.A. and are used by permission.

Cover design: Ellen Maly
Text design: David Lott

The Library of Congress has cataloged the first four volumes of Series A as follows:

Proclamation 6, Series A: interpreting the lessons of the church
    year.
            p.   cm.
        Contents: [1] Advent/Christmas / J. Christiaan Beker — [2]
    Epiphany / Susan K. Hedahl — [3] Lent / Peter J. Gomes — [4] Holy
    Week / Robin Scroggs.
        ISBN 0-8006-4207-4 (v. 1 : alk. paper) — ISBN 0-8006-4208-2 (v.
    2 : alk. paper) — ISBN 0-8006-4209-0 (v. 3 : alk. paper) — ISBN 0-8006-4210-4
    (v. 4 : alk. paper).
        1. Bible—Homiletical use. 2. Bible—liturgical lessons,
    English.
    BS534.5P74   1995
    251—dc20   95-4622
                                                           CIP
            Series B:
            Advent/Christmas / Arthur J. Dewey—ISBN 0-8006-4215-5
            Epiphany / Mark Allan Powell—ISBN 0-8006-4216-3
            Lent / James H. Harris, Miles Jerome Jones, and Jerome C. Ross—
                ISBN 0-8006-4217-1
            Holy Week / Philip H. Pfatteicher—ISBN 0-8006-4218-X
            Easter / Beverly R. Gaventa—ISBN 0-8006-4219-8
            Pentecost 1 / Ched Myers—ISBN 0-8006-4220-1
            Pentecost 2 / Richard L. Eslinger—ISBN 0-8006-4221-X
            Pentecost 3 / Laura Lagerquist-Gottwald and Norman K. Gottwald—
                ISBN 0-8006-4222-8

The paper used in this publication meets the minimum requirements of American National
Standard for Information Sciences—Permanence of Paper for Printed Library Materials,
ANSI Z329.48-1948.

Manufactured in the U. S. A.   AF 1-4216

00   99   98   97   96   1   2   3   4   5   6   7   8   9   10

Contents

For
The Reverend J. Roderick Rinell, Jr.

The Epiphany of Our Lord

Lectionary	First Lesson	Psalm	Second Lesson	Gospel
Revised Common	Isa. 60:1-6	Ps. 72:1-7, 10-14	Eph. 3:1-12	Matt. 2:1-12
Episcopal (BCP)	Isa. 60:1-6, 9	Ps. 72:1-2, 10-17 or Psalm 72	Eph. 3:1-12	Matt. 2:1-12
Roman Catholic	Isa. 60:1-6	Ps. 72:1-2, 7-8, 10-13	Eph. 3:2-3a, 5-6	Matt. 2:1-12
Lutheran (LBW)	Isa. 60:1-6	Psalm 72	Eph. 3:2-12	Matt. 2:1-12

Persons who have access to previously published books in this series of *Proclamation: Aids for Interpreting the Lessons of the Church Year* should note that the lessons for this day are treated in the "Epiphany" volume for each year (not just Series B).

FIRST LESSON: ISAIAH 60:1-9

The epiphany theme established in our Gospel reading for today is sounded in this passage in a way that goes well beyond the superficial connection suggested by the mention of gold and frankincense in v. 6. The prophet describes the destiny of Israel as being to provide light for a dark world (vv. 2-3), thus seizing upon a metaphor that later writers would apply to both Jesus (John 1:5; 8:12) and the church (Matt. 5:14-16).

As expressed in this passage, the vision of Israel as light for the world has two essential parts. One is *restoration of family*, a reunion that includes the return of children who have wandered or been taken away (vv. 4, 9). Another is *expansion of family*, inclusion of people from many nations who come to Israel from all directions, by land (vv. 6-7), by sea (vv. 5, 9), and even by air (v. 8)!

Scholars attribute this prophecy to Third Isaiah, though much of the oracle recalls earlier sayings from the Isaianic school (for instance, 2:2-3; 9:2; 58:10b). The message, then, is not new, but the context in which it is to be heard is different. Isaiah of Jerusalem called Israel to trust in God during the Assyrian crisis of the eighth century B.C.E. Second Isaiah proclaimed a message of comfort and hope during the exile in Babylon two hundred years later. Now, the time of exile is ending and the return to the homeland has begun.

Why does this prophet believe it is important for the returning exiles to recall the universal vision? First, the vision will prevent any half-hearted acceptance of reality that may derive from cynicism or apathy. The exiles are returning to a despoiled land where the temple lies in ruins, the people are divided, and the economy is in chaos. Third Isaiah addresses this crisis of disappointment by recalling the glorious vision that sustained the people through their hard times and encouraging them to settle for nothing less. What is happening now must be understood within the full context of God's promises and interpreted from a perspective that appreciates the tension between what is *already* and *not yet*. The return from exile is indeed the work of God and a fulfillment of promise, the moment for which they have been waiting all their lives. But for those who return, look around, and ask, "Is this all?" the answer is, "No! Remember the vision! There is more."

Second, the prophet does not allow for any prioritization between the two aspects of the vision, restoration and expansion. The returning exiles are not to think, "First we will get our own house in order and then we will see about becoming a light to the nations." In this text, in fact, that chronology is reversed: *first*, nations come to Israel's light (v. 3); *then*, Israel's sons and daughters come from afar (v. 4). Indeed, a rather remarkable connection between the restoration and expansion themes is made in v. 9, where it appears that the latter facilitates the former. The children do not simply come back to the homeland of their own accord but are brought by representatives of the nations who now revere the Holy One of Israel.

SECOND LESSON: EPHESIANS 3:1-12

Insight into mysteries was a popular theme in the world that produced our New Testament. Witness the prevalence of apocalyptic writings, of gnostic literature, and of secrecy themes in documents like the Gospel of Mark and the scrolls at Qumran! The author of Ephesians (either Paul or someone writing in his name) exploits this interest to rhetorical advantage in the pericope for today, a text that claims to reveal God's "eternal purpose" (v. 11) for all of history.

The writer entices his audience, teasing them about the significance of what he is about to say (vv. 3-5). A mystery has been revealed to him. In former generations, this mystery was not known to anyone at all, and even now it has only been revealed by the Spirit to a select few—to holy apostles and prophets. But he is going to tell *us*. Then, finally, in v. 6, he does: the mystery is that "Gentiles have become fellow heirs, members of the same body, and sharers in the same promise in Christ Jesus through the gospel."

After such a big build-up, this may seem anticlimactic, especially for an audience of Gentile Christians (3:1) who we would expect already know that the gospel is for them. But there is more to it than that. A couple of theological points are scored here that are subtle but significant.

First, the author claims this is a new revelation, unknown in "former generations" (v. 5) even though he knows that Old Testament prophets spoke about the inclusion of Gentiles in the people of God (he quotes some of these references at other points in the epistle, for example, Isa. 57:19 in 2:17). What this writer envisions is not the inclusion of Gentiles in an entity that remains "Israel," but the creation of a new multicultural community. Such a vision is qualitatively different from that which is typically projected in Old Testament accounts, including the verses from Third Isaiah that form our first lesson for today. In Romans 11, Paul likens the inclusion of Gentiles to the grafting of a branch onto a tree. In Ephesians, however, another metaphor is used, one that is also Pauline (Rom. 12:4-5; 1 Cor. 12:12-13). Jews and Gentiles are "members of the same body" (v. 6), and thus equally integral to its identity and necessary for its survival. Indeed, the nature of this unity is emphasized in v. 6 by three words that begin with a form of the prefix *syn-* ("together"), all three of which relate to concepts discussed elsewhere in Ephesians: *sygklēronoma* ("fellow heirs," 1:14, 18); *syssōma* ("members of the same body," 1:22-23); and, *symmetocha* ("sharers in the promise," 2:12).

Second, the formation of this community is not presented as one part of some overarching scheme or as a step toward the accomplishment of some divine plan but as, definitively, the fulfillment of God's eternal purpose. The creation of multicultural communities is often viewed as a high priority today also, but few proponents of such communities would elevate their significance to the level that this writer does. We might be more inclined, for instance, to identify God's ultimate purpose as the gracious salvation of humans and to view the formation of a multicultural church as the appropriate and necessary means through which this purpose may be carried out. The writer to the Ephesians would reverse these priorities: salvation is the means and the formation of the community is the end. The reason God has decided to provide salvation by grace is so that all may be placed on the same footing (2:8-9). Common dependence upon grace is intended to facilitate transcendence of cultural and ethnic barriers to the unification of humanity.

The final verses of this pericope identify Paul (vv. 7-9) and the church (vv. 10-12) as servants of God's grace entrusted with revealing this mystery. Specifically, Paul's task is to reveal the mystery to people ("everyone," v. 9) and the church's calling is to reveal it to spiritual beings ("rulers and authorities in the heavenly places," v. 10). The implication of the latter formulation is that not even angels or demons are able to understand the mystery that is here revealed. They may regard the gift of salvation as capricious and wonder what divine purpose the death and resurrection of Christ is expected to further. But when the church becomes the inclusive community that God intends it to be, the method of God's madness will become apparent to them. The wisdom of God, which is itself *polypoikilos* (v. 10, "multicolored" or "richly varied"), will be made known to them.

GOSPEL: MATTHEW 2:1-12

The story of the Magi recalls elements from the narrative of Balaam in the Old Testament (Numbers 22–24). According to Philo and the *Palestinian Targum*, Balaam and his two servants were regarded as magi. Like the Magi in Matthew 2, they travel to Palestine from the east. A wicked king attempts to use them to destroy God's people, but informed of God's will through the intervention of an angel, they offer blessing and worship instead. In Num. 24:17, Balaam even refers to a star that he sees rising out of Jacob.

The story also foreshadows later developments in Matthew's narrative. Even in infancy Jesus inspires both worship and hostile opposition, responses that are repeated throughout the narrative. The Magi represent the first of many characters to worship Jesus in Matthew (2:11; compare 8:2; 9:18; 14:33; 15:25; 20:20; 28:9, 17), a point that may be obscured in English Bibles that choose a soft translation here for *proskyneō* (NRSV, "do homage"). According to Matt. 4:10, *proskyneō* describes devotion that is to be shown to God alone. Thus, the attribution of worship (*proskyneō*) to Jesus here and elsewhere in Matthew has christological significance, marking Jesus as the one in whom God is present (1:23). As for opposition, the religious leaders of Israel here do the bidding of a political ruler who wishes to destroy Jesus. Later the situation will be ironically reversed: the political ruler (Pilate) will do the bidding of religious leaders who have decided Jesus must die (27:1-2, 11-26).

A literary masterpiece, this brief episode in Matthew's story has captured the imagination of Christians for centuries and inspired the formation of numerous legends. The Magi came to be identified as kings, probably due to an association of this passage with Isa. 60:3, part of our first lesson for today. They came to be called "wise men," an identification so pervasive that it is even used in English translations of the Bible (including NRSV). In the Middle Ages, the Western Church decided there were three Magi (the Eastern Church has twelve) and assigned them names: Caspar, Melchior, and Balthasar.

Such legends are not insignificant for Christian piety, but they may distract us from the story Matthew tells. Matthew's story is indeed about kings and wise men, but these figures are people other than the Magi. The *kings* in Matthew 2 are Herod and Jesus. Herod exemplifies the sort of king whom Jesus later denounces in Matt. 20:25. He is a tyrant who lords over those he rules rather than serving them. He is not a ruler who "shepherds" God's people (v. 6). By contrast, the infant king Jesus is helpless and vulnerable, a ruler whose power is hidden in humility (compare 21:5). The *wise men* in Matthew 2 are the chief priests and the scribes who function as Herod's key advisors. Learned in the Scriptures, they possess academic knowledge that both Herod and the Magi lack. But what good does it do them? It does not lead them to their Messiah but causes them to become involved in a plot to kill him.

Responsible exegesis by both Catholics and Protestants has always resisted the identification of the Magi as kings. Calvin called it "dubious" and Luther polemicized against the tale in harmony (for once) with doctors of the Roman Church. But the identification of the Magi as "wise men" may ultimately be even more problematic because a major theme in Matthew is that God does not reveal things to "the wise and intelligent" (11:25). This withholding of revelation is evident here with regard to the chief priests and scribes. Elsewhere in Matthew's infancy narrative, God intervenes to prevent characters from inadvertently doing the wrong thing. Joseph is told not to divorce his wife (1:20) and the Magi are warned not to reveal Jesus' whereabouts to Herod (2:12). But no dream or angel comes to these wise men of Israel and, lacking divine guidance, their wisdom and knowledge becomes a tool for evil.

If the Magi are not kings or wise men, what are they? In Matthew's narrative, kings are contrasted with *servants* (20:25-28) and wise men are contrasted with *infants* (11:25). The Magi are depicted in Matthew 2 as persons who do as they are instructed, who seek no honor for themselves, and who gladly humble themselves, kneeling even before a woman and a child. Clearly, they fit the image of servants better than that of kings. Surprisingly, they also embody perfectly the two traits that are ascribed to infants in Matthew's story. They are persons to whom God reveals what is hidden (11:25) and from whom God derives worship or praise (21:16). If Jesus as a literal infant is contrasted here with Herod, the Magi as metaphorical infants may be contrasted with Herod's advisors, the wise men of Israel.

In short, the central message of this text may be framed as an answer to the question, Whom does God favor? *Not* kings or wise men, but the Magi who embody qualities that this Gospel will declare antithetical to the traits of the royal and the wise. Ironically, in recasting the story so that the Magi actually become kings or wise men, readers have subverted this message until the text seems to support notions it was intended to suppress. We must not be arrogant in judging these traditions too harshly. They tell us that, apart from such elaboration, the message of this text has been a hard one to hear. It still is.

CONNECTIONS

The English word *epiphany* derives from the Greek *epiphaneia*, which means "appearance" or "appearing." In a religious sense, the term is used for manifestations of divinity on earth and, in the Bible, it is used exclusively for Christ (with reference to his first appearance, 2 Tim. 1:10; with reference to his second coming, 2 Thess. 2:8; 1 Tim. 6:14; 2 Tim. 4:1, 8; Titus 2:13).

Liturgically, the day of Epiphany has been a time for the church to celebrate God's manifestation in Christ. The scriptural focus has always been on events where that manifestation became public: the birth of Jesus, his baptism, his first miracle (water into wine), or his transfiguration. Today, the Eastern Church celebrates the baptism of Jesus on the day of Epiphany, while the Western Church focuses on the visit of the Magi, observing other epiphany events on Sundays during the season that follows.

The common theme in the three lessons appointed for this day is the manifestation of God to people outside the religious community. Third Isaiah reminds the community of its call to be a light to the nations and destroys the false dichotomy between internal and external ministry by suggesting that expansion and restoration are integrally connected. The author of Ephesians suggests that the ultimate purpose of God is the unification of humanity in a truly multicultural community where all distinctions between "insiders" and "outsiders" have vanished. The Gospel of Matthew reminds us that such distinctions began to erode with the coming of Christ, who was revealed to some who were thought to be on the outside and paradoxically rejected by many who were thought to be on the inside.

The church's observance of Epiphany ought not be a triumphal occasion for those who have seen the light to celebrate their privileged status. The lessons appointed for this day encourage humble admission that God's glory may be manifested where we least expect it. Sometimes God's people become light for others (Isa. 60:3; Eph. 3:10); sometimes they appear blind to the light others can see (Matt. 2:1-6). But always, the light is there, as God graciously, mysteriously, and defiantly breaks into our lives. The effect of God's epiphany is to transform human community by uniting people throughout the world into one family, one body that has access to God through faith (Eph. 3:12). In this light we worship and our worship is marked by confidence, boldness, and joy (Isa. 60:5; Eph. 3:12; Matt. 2:10).

First Sunday after the Epiphany
The Baptism of Our Lord

Lectionary	First Lesson	Psalm	Second Lesson	Gospel
Revised Common	Gen. 1:1-5	Psalm 29	Acts 19:1-7	Mark 1:4-11
Episcopal (BCP)	Isa. 42:1-9	Ps. 89:1-29 *or* 20-29	Acts 10:34-38	Mark 1:7-11
Roman Catholic	Isa. 42:1-4, 6-7	Ps. 29:1-4, 9-11	Acts 10:34-38	Mark 1:7-11
Lutheran (LBW)	Isa. 42:1-7	Ps. 45:7-9	Acts 10:34-38	Mark 1:4-11

FIRST LESSON: GENESIS 1:1-5

In his mammoth commentary on *Genesis 1–11* (Minneapolis: Fortress Press, 1994), Claus Westermann comments on the profundity of the Bible's first verse: "When one has said that creation is the work of God, then one has said everything that there is to say about it" (p. 97). All things—*all things*—are by definition godly, inextricably linked to God and to each other. Significantly, the God who creates is not described here as the "God of Israel" or as the first person of the Christian Trinity but as God "without any limiting point of reference" (Ludwig Köhler, *Old Testament Theology,* [Philadelphia: Westminster Press, 1957], 21).

We cannot determine with certainty whether this first verse is to be read as an independent sentence, as in the RSV ("God created"), or as a dependent clause, as in the NRSV ("when God created"). Either translation is possible syntactically. More important is the recognition that, even if 1:1 is an independent sentence, it serves as a heading to introduce the topic of creation rather than as a description of the first act of creation. We would be very wrong to think that, first, God creates the heavens and the earth (1:1) and, then, sets to work on the formless void that has come into being. The God of the Bible is not described as creating (and then refining) chaos. In the Bible, creation and chaos are antithetical.

This means that Genesis 1 does not describe a creation *ex nihilo* ("out of nothing"). Where we pick up the story, some things already exist—darkness, the deep, waters, even the formless void that is to become the earth (v. 2). We need not regard the doctrine of creation *ex nihilo* as wrong or even as unbiblical (see John 1:3) to recognize that it is not the concern of this passage. Genesis 1 does not offer an account of the beginning of "the universe," but of time, that is, of history. According to the Bible, darkness and chaos predate time, but so does God.

God creates light (v. 3) even before the sun, moon, and stars (1:16) and immediately separates this light from the darkness. Creation and separation will be closely linked in the next two acts of creation also (1:6-9), to the degree that some have even suggested that God initially creates *by separating*, that is, by bringing order to the chaos. Indeed the word for "create" used in 1:1 (*bara*) probably derives from a root form that means "to cut (separate)."

For the priestly writers, this separation is confirmed by *defining*, so here God names the light and the darkness (v. 5). Naming or defining is an essential element (some would say *the* essential element) in the next two acts also (1:8, 10) and becomes significant again in the story of Adam and Eve (2:19- 20, 3:20). What is important here is that God names both the light and the darkness, even though in v. 4, God declared the light alone to be good. The darkness is not described as created by God or as good, but it is defined by God and so becomes part of God's created order. Many theological analogies could be found to this understanding of light and darkness, including that of life and death. By creating life and declaring it to be good God also takes dominion over death which, though it is not good in and of itself, is now redeemed as a part of God's good creation.

We note, finally, that God's word is what brings about creation (compare John 1:1-5). The power to create does not lie in the word as such (which would be a magical conception) but in the activity of God speaking. The God of the Bible is revealed through word and deed, so that to believe in God is fundamentally to believe in what God says and does (as opposed to believing in "God" as an abstract idea). Genesis 1 is concerned with preserving the distinction between the Creator and creation, but at the same time, indicates that the word of God transcends this distinction. As Dietrich Bonhoeffer says, "the only continuity between God and God's work is the Word" (*Creation and Fall* [London: SCM, 1959], 19).

SECOND LESSON: ACTS 19:1-7

This story represents the first episode in Luke's account of Paul's ministry at Ephesus, which in Acts serves as the grand finale to the latter's illustrious missionary career. We might wish for more information that would provide background for understanding the Corinthian correspondence Paul produced during his three years at Ephesus or, at least, some details concerning the afflictions and dangers that, according to that correspondence, he experienced while there (1 Cor. 15:32; 2 Cor. 1:8). Instead, Luke focuses in Acts 19 on the development of the Christian movement as distinct from other sects that honored Jesus (vv. 1-7), from synagogal Judaism (vv.

8-10), from folk religion or magic (vv. 11-20) and from what he must have regarded as pure paganism (vv. 21-41).

The episode narrated here is linked closely to that which precedes it (Acts 18:24-28). We are probably expected to regard the Ephesian disciples whom Paul encounters as members of the same group to which Apollos belonged, since like him they "knew only the baptism of John" (18:25; 19:3). But these Ephesians are not disciples of John. In Luke and Acts the term *disciples* (v. 1) always means "disciples of Jesus," just as the term *believers* (v. 2) always means "believers in Jesus." The anomaly here is that these people, like Apollos, consider themselves to be what we would call Christians even though they have never received Christian baptism.

The consequence of this deficiency is spelled out in today's text: They have not received the Holy Spirit. The response to Paul's question in 19:2 should not be exaggerated to imply that these disciples have never heard of the Holy Spirit. Anyone who knew the Scriptures (e.g., Isa. 63:10-11; Joel 2:28-29) and certainly anyone who had heard the preaching of John (Luke 3:16) knew of God's promise to give the Holy Spirit to people. When the Ephesian disciples say, "We have not even heard that there is a Holy Spirit," they mean that they have not heard the Spirit is available—they do not know the promise has been fulfilled.

The remedy for this lack is baptism in the name of Jesus. Sacramental churches should not jump on this passage too quickly as a proof text for demonstrating that the Holy Spirit is (always) given in baptism since, (*a*) other passages in Acts portray the gift of the Spirit as an event occurring before baptism (10:44) or completely separate from baptism (8:15-17); and, (*b*) a case could be made even here for the Spirit being given through the laying on of hands that follows baptism rather than through baptism itself (19:6; compare 8:18-19). Still, there can be no doubt that baptism in the name of Jesus and the gift of the Holy Spirit are expected to go together. The instances from Acts 8 and 10 just referenced are reported precisely because they are anomalous. Luke preserves such stories to insure that the church remembers the Holy Spirit is God's to give as God directs, not (as Simon Magus thinks in 8:19) the property of the church to give according to its prescription. But, this said, Paul's question in 19:3 clearly indicates a normative expectation that people who have been baptized in the name of Jesus will have received the Holy Spirit.

Other details of this passage need not detain us. The glossolalia and prophesying (v. 6) recall Pentecost (2:4, 11) and the outpouring of the Spirit on Gentiles in Acts 10:45-46. Thus, we are assured that now the Ephesian disciples are no longer sectarian but have been brought into line with the experience of the whole church. The number of the disciples (v. 7) is probably not intended to imply anything apostolic, since it is approximate (*about* twelve).

GOSPEL: MARK 1:4-11

The setting for this first episode in Mark's narrative is "the wilderness," an ambiguous locale that could be viewed as a waterless place haunted by demons and wild animals (Deut. 8:15; Matt. 12:43) or as a retreat to which God's people are called for spiritual bonding (Hos. 2:14). Both meanings apply in Mark 1:12-13, the verses immediately following this text. Here, the wilderness is clearly not waterless, but that is because the Jordan marks its boundary. Through these waters, people leave the wilderness and enter into the promised land (Joshua 3). Most notably, the wilderness is the place where the way of the Lord is to be prepared (Isa. 40:3; Mark 1:3) and, hence, is a focal point for eschatological hope. John the Baptizer's appearance in the wilderness in the guise of a prophet (Zech. 13:4)—indeed, Elijah! (2 Kings 1:8)—is intended to inspire such hope (Mal. 3:5; Mark 9:11-13).

John's ministry consists of "proclaiming a baptism of repentance for the forgiveness of sins" (v. 4). In this context, repentance means turning toward God to embrace the new age of salvation that is dawning, an age marked by forgiveness of sins. Of course, such repentance also implies turning away from all that is evil and ungodly, but the point here is not simply that God will forgive the sins of those who repent. That would be nothing new. In Mark's Gospel, John's baptism does not symbolize repentance as an instance of human determination but as a gift of God. In Matthew and in Luke, this baptism may be withheld until some evidence of a changed life has been produced (Matt. 3:7-10; Luke 3:7-14). But here, God's grace is displayed dramatically in that the people enter the promise of forgiveness through baptismal waters, actually *confessing their sins* as they go (1:5). Mark does not portray baptism as a symbolic cleansing of the penitent from the guilt of past sins, but as an act that conveys the gift of repentance and forgiveness to current sinners. We may note, of course, that Mark is collapsing the historical distinctions preserved in Acts between the baptism of John and baptism in the name of Jesus. Mark essentially presents John's baptism as a type of Christian baptism. Since he does not go on to narrate the history of the church, this is his only chance to portray his image of what baptism should be.

The words of John in vv. 7-8 contain a double meaning. On one level, the "more powerful" one who is coming is the Lord God, whose way John has come to prepare (1:3). God, then, is the one who "will baptize you [plural] with the Holy Spirit." But this promise is only partially fulfilled in what follows, for when God does arrive, tearing the heavens, God baptizes only one member of the crowd with the Holy Spirit, Jesus from Nazareth (1:9-10). As the narrative continues, however, we will be led to recognize that Jesus himself is to be regarded as the more powerful one, as the Lord, and as the one who will baptize us all with the Holy Spirit.

This descent of the Spirit recalls the creation account in our first lesson. In fact, the word for the Spirit's activity employed in Gen. 1:2 suggests the movement of a bird, as is indicated by the REB translation, "hovered." The Babylonian Talmud is specific: "the Spirit of God was brooding on the face of the waters *like a dove*." Thus, the baptism of Jesus may be a private epiphany in Mark's Gospel (apparently only Jesus sees and hears what happens), but it signifies nothing less than the dawn of the new creation. The tearing of the heavens (only in Mark) is surely an apocalyptic event, indicating that from this point on the division of the divine and human realms has been irreparably breeched. Thus is fulfilled the hope of the prophet, "O that you would tear open the heavens and come down" (Isa. 64:1). Because of what he sees on this day, Jesus is able to declare (in our Gospel lesson for the Third Sunday after the Epiphany) that God's reign is now a present reality (Mark 1:15).

Mark tells the story of Jesus' baptism in a way that parallels the story of his death at the end of the Gospel (15:37-39). In the baptism account, the heavens rip, the Spirit comes to Jesus, and a voice declares that he is God's son. In the passion narrative, the curtain in the temple tears, the spirit (NRSV, "breath") leaves Jesus, and another voice proclaims, "Truly this man was the Son of God!" The connection between these stories is even closer when we realize that the curtain in the temple was in fact a pictorial tapestry displaying "a panorama of the entire heavens," as Josephus puts it. To be sure we don't miss the connection (though many have), Mark even has Jesus explicitly refer to his death as his baptism in 10:38.

What is the point of such a parallel? Perhaps Mark wants to suggest that baptism is like death (compare Rom. 6:3-11). Through both, God's people enter into a realm of new life and experience the new creation. Announcing the present and eternal dimensions of this new life is tantamount to "proclaiming a baptism of repentance for the forgiveness of sins."

CONNECTIONS

Lectionaries have often paired the story of Jesus' baptism with the first few verses of Isaiah 42, a connection that emphasizes the character of the person who receives the spirit of the Lord. This is not the best companion text, especially when the Gospel lesson is drawn from Mark's account, where character is not an issue. The baptism of John does not transform sinners into nonsinners or even heavy sinners into light sinners. It reorients those who acknowledge their sins to the reign of grace marked by God's forgiveness. The descent of the Spirit on Jesus does not serve to make him a better person but to empower him to proclaim the present reality of God's reign in word and deed. Obviously, Jesus' baptism is unique in certain respects, but it is also paradigmatic. As John's words testify, Jesus is not only the one who receives God's baptism of Spirit, but also the one who will baptize others with this Holy Spirit. Thus, the baptism of Jesus marks the beginning of a new age. The advent of God's rule is so significant that its establishment can only be compared to the reordering of chaos at the beginning of time. The descent of the Spirit at Jesus' baptism initiates a new creation and so indicates that the reign of grace is now in effect.

The story of the Ephesian disciples ties into this theme nicely also, for it indicates that, in a manner analogous to what happened to Jesus at his baptism, the Holy Spirit comes to those who are baptized in the name of Jesus. The Christian movement is not ultimately about being a disciple of Jesus in the sense of believing facts about him and committing to live in accord with his teaching. It is about living in the new creation as people who have been filled with God's Holy Spirit. We should be careful, though, not to preach this in a way that promotes an ideology of "successful living," at least not as our culture usually defines success. Rather, as the whole of Mark's Gospel and the book of Acts both make clear, the power of Spirit-filled living is always directed toward the accomplishment of God's agenda (and here the Isaiah 42 text would have been helpful). The baptized devote themselves to serving others and to working for God's justice and righteousness.

Second Sunday after the Epiphany
Second Sunday in Ordinary Time

Lectionary	First Lesson	Psalm	Second Lesson	Gospel
Revised Common	I Sam. 3:1-10 (11-20)	Ps. 139:1-6, 13-18	I Cor. 6:12-20	John 1:43-51
Episcopal (BCP)	I Sam. 3:1-10	Ps. 63:1-8	I Cor. 6:11b-20	John 1:43-51
Roman Catholic	I Sam. 3:3b-10, 19	Ps. 40:2, 4, 7-10	I Cor. 6:13c-15a, 17-20	John 1:35-42
Lutheran (LBW)	I Sam. 3:1-10	Psalm 67	I Cor. 6:12-20	John 1:43-51

FIRST LESSON: I SAMUEL 3:1-10 (11-20)

This narrative describes the transfer of power from the priestly house of Eli to the chosen prophet Samuel. If we consider the first ten verses only, we are left with an extended build-up to a message from the Lord that breaks off at the climactic point just as that message is about to be spoken. In the verses that follow, God speaks a harsh word of judgment against the house of Eli that clarifies why it is now Samuel and not Eli to whom God speaks.

The first part of the story evinces a certain charm that derives from the skill with which it is told. The setting or mood is established as a time of transition, marked by decline and need for renewal. Eli's eyes have "begun to grow dim" (v. 2). The lamp of God has "not yet gone out" (v. 3). Such references symbolize a period of "fading" rather than total darkness. The word of the Lord is rare (v. 1) but not, as we soon learn, totally absent. The threefold call that follows (vv. 4-8) builds suspense, and Samuel's repeated failure to recognize its source adds a touch of humor and irony. These elements are not merely ornamental: the reader is expected to note the persistence of God and to observe that only Samuel hears God's voice, two points significant for interpretation.

A traditional approach to this text focuses on the character of the boy Samuel. He is not a member of Eli's family, but a young assistant. Born to a barren woman as an answer to prayer, he was dedicated to temple service from his birth (1 Sam. 1:1—2:11). The attitude he expresses in v. 10 ("Speak, for your servant is listening") presents the ideal response to God (compare Luke 1:38). Thus, Samuel is a servant who ministers to the Lord (2:11) and who finds favor with the Lord and with people (2:26). He is contrasted with the sons of Eli, "scoundrels" who have no regard for the Lord or for people (2:12-13). The Lord's choice of Samuel over these official leaders reveals how God evaluates credentials for leadership. As Samuel himself will later state, "the LORD does not see as mortals see . . . the LORD looks on the heart" (1 Sam. 16:7).

A somewhat different approach may focus on the more complex character of Eli. The judgment of God announced in 3:11-14 (and previously in 2:27-36) is against him as well as his evil sons. He is to blame because "he did not restrain them" (3:13). Still, we may feel some sympathy for this old priest, who had at least objected to his sons' behavior (2:23-25) and who, even now, submits himself to the will of God (3:18). The judgment against him is mitigated insofar as he calls Samuel "my son" (3:6, 16). His physical descendants will not inherit his mantle as priest and prophet of God, but one whom he regards as his son will.

The most important message of this text, however, is found in the theme of divine persistence. Sermons that extol the example of Samuel as a model of readiness may miss the portrait of God as aggressive initiator. God's people are not allowed to go wanting. God finds a way to meet their needs, sometimes through what appear to be surprising or desperate measures. If God's people need a prophet, God will find them one, even if it means calling a child who does "not yet know the LORD" (v. 7). When light is fading but not yet gone, God enters the dimness of human existence. When God's agents fail, when all that is sacred seems profane and the word of the Lord is rare, God does things that "make both ears of anyone who hears of it tingle" (v. 11). When God's call goes unheeded, God calls again, and again. The moral of the story is, God will not be deterred. God will find a way.

SECOND LESSON: I CORINTHIANS 6:12-20

Paul's letters to the Corinthians would be easier to understand if we had copies of the letters that they had sent to him (see 1 Cor. 5:9; 2 Cor. 2:3-4, 7:8). In this portion of the letter, Paul appears to cite slogans that the Corinthians have quoted to him and then respond to these slogans. The issue is whether Christians are expected to refrain from using prostitutes, whose services were readily available and often socially acceptable in the Greco-Roman world. As we reconstruct the dialogue between Paul and the Corinthians on this matter, we gain insight not only into ethics of sexuality (and ethics generally), but also into two theological propositions that form the basis for Paul's thinking: the doctrine of Christian freedom and the unity of the human being.

Slogan One: "All things are lawful for me" (v. 12, and 10:23). Paul himself speaks of Christians as being free from the law (Rom. 10:4; Gal. 4:7), so perhaps the Corinthians think he will have to accept this point. He does not, for Paul does not define freedom in terms of what is permissiblebut in terms of what is helpful (Gal. 5:13). Otherwise, freedom is illusory. Sexual license is not a sign of freedom from the law but of slavery to desires.

Slogan Two: "Food is meant for the stomach and the stomach for food" (v. 13). The Corinthians' argument here is probably intended to draw an analogy between hunger and sexual desire: both are natural appetites that need to be satisfied. The comparison is obviously flawed since people need food but not sex to survive, but Paul doesn't waste time pointing this out. Rather than attacking the analogy itself, he undermines the assumption that undergirds it by citing a slogan of his own: "The body is meant not for fornication but for the Lord, and the Lord for the body" (v. 13). Our intended (and therefore most natural) function is to live in ways that serve the Lord. Paul would not even agree with the statement that "the stomach is for food," if this were used to justify gluttony.

Slogan Three: "Every sin that a person commits is outside the body" (v. 18—these words should probably be in quotation marks). In citing these words to Paul, the Corinthians meant to say that sin is a spiritual matter. What one does with one's body is irrelevant if it does not affect the soul or spirit. This was also the point in the earlier remark that the stomach and food are just two things God will destroy (v. 13). If the body is transient, we don't need to be concerned about it. Paul objects on several accounts: (*a*) our bodies are not transient but are destined to be raised (albeit transformed) from the dead (v. 14, compare 15:35-53); (*b*) our bodies make up the body of Christ on earth (v. 15, compare 12:27); (*c*) our bodies are the abode of the Holy Spirit (v. 19); (*d*) our bodies belong to God, having been "bought with a price" (v. 20).

Historical distance allows us to see why Paul and the Corinthian Christians were at odds over this matter. Paul rejected the radical dualism of body and soul that informed Greek thought in favor of the Hebraic perspective that views the human being as a unified entity. The Greek view, of course, prevails in our own culture and often goes unchallenged even in communities committed to the Bible. The excesses of the Corinthians are usually attacked as just that, rather than as ramifications of an unbiblical anthropology. Paul's understanding enables him to argue for sexual morality positively, not by demeaning the human body by presenting sex as "dirty," but by claiming that "the Lord is for the body" (v. 12).

We must note one potential failing in Paul's approach, granting of course that he cannot attend to everything at once. He appears to regard prostitutes as a source of evil and temptation to Christians but he betrays no concern (here) for the prostitutes themselves. In this respect, his attitude differs markedly from that of Jesus (Luke 7:36-50).

GOSPEL: JOHN 1:43-51

This lesson is read with a focus on either discipleship or Christology. When the former is emphasized, the story may present a paradigm for personal evangelism. A chain of witness is established as Jesus finds Philip (v. 43) who, in turn, finds Nathanael (v. 45). The invitation to "Come and see" recalls Ps. 34:8 and is more effective than any argument might have been. These points are more dramatic when the prior passage is considered, for there we see a similar chain of witness (1:35-37, 40-41) and an identical invitation (1:39).

Nathanael may be regarded as a type of true Israel, as a figure who demonstrates the ideal Jewish response. Jesus describes him as "an Israelite in whom there is no deceit" (v. 47) and he acclaims Jesus as "King of Israel" (v. 49). The curious saying in v. 51 recalls a scene from Gen. 28:12, with Nathanael in the role of Jacob, the one who first bore the name "Israel." Since Jacob was widely known as a deceiver (Genesis 27), Jesus' description of Nathanael in v. 47 may provide a contrast between the old Israel and the new.

If we regard Nathanael as an idealized figure, we will have to rethink two negative features sometimes ascribed to him. He is neither bigoted nor presumptuous. The question Nathanael poses in v. 46 does not reflect an arrogant disparagement of Jesus' small town origins but, rather, devotion to Scripture (compare John 7:52). Nathanael is right to question whether "the one about whom Moses in the law and also the prophets wrote" (v. 45) can come from Nazareth, which is never mentioned in the Old Testament (or the Talmud or Midrash, for that matter). The ideal Israelite knows Scripture and looks for its proper fulfillment, but is also willing to "come and see," to be open to whatever God may do.

Likewise, Jesus' response to Nathanael's acclamation of faith (vv. 49-50) is not a rebuke, as many take it. John's Gospel is written so that people may come to believe what Nathanael here professes (20:31). The point here is not that Nathanael offers an overblown confession out of keeping with the little evidence he has received; the point rather is that as one prepared he comes to faith easily. According to John's Gospel, people should not need signs to believe (4:48), but signs are offered that they might believe (20:30-31). Jesus is impressed that for Nathanael great signs were not necessary, though he will see them nevertheless. Thus, Nathanael may be compared to Thomas who, at the end of the story offers a similar confession based on the greatest sign of all (20:27-29). Nathanael may be the prototype for those who come to believe even when they have not seen such signs (20:29).

When the focus of interpretation is placed on Christology, much may be made of the titles for Jesus that accumulate here: "him about whom Moses in the law and also the prophets wrote" (v. 45); "Son of God" (v. 49); "King of Israel" (v. 49); and "Son of Man" (v. 51). To these may be added "Lamb of God" (1:36) and "Messiah" (1:41) from the preceding material. Commentaries are filled with discussion as to whether these should be read incrementally (so that Jesus' self-designation, "Son of Man," is climactic) or linked to the categories that John the Baptist denies for himself in 1:19-21.

The verse that evokes the most comment is 1:51. The most natural interpretation identifies Jesus with the ladder of Jacob's vision (Gen. 28:12). Less likely suggestions identify Jesus (rather than Nathanael) with Jacob so that the angels are ascending and descending to him rather than literally on him, or identify Jesus with Bethel ("house of God"), the place of Jacob's vision. In any case, the dominant theme appears to be that Jesus is the mediator between heaven and earth, the link between the human and the divine realms. Recognizing this has existential significance that goes beyond what may be expressed by any or all of the titles that accrue to him in this chapter.

The emphasis in the story as a whole is on Jesus' ability to know things, as exemplified in his seeing Nathanael under the fig tree even though he was not physically present at the time (v. 48). The latter action is not as superficial as it might appear, but has spiritual implications (compare 4:19, 29). It ties into the themes of "knowing" and "seeing" developed throughout this Gospel. Ironically, Nathanael is invited to "come and see," but when he does come, he discovers that he has been seen. Nathanael does not come to know Jesus, as modern evangelical parlance puts it, but comes to be known by him. Like the woman at the well in John 4, he is willing to put his faith in the one who knows him.

CONNECTIONS

A common theme for the day, found in both the first lesson and the Gospel reading, is that of the divine call. The second lesson, as is often the case, pursues a course of its own.

Samuel is a biblical figure about whom much is written, but today's lesson is interested only in his selection by God, not his later achievements. Nathanael is one of whom we know almost nothing except his call, though a subsequent mention in John 21:2 assures us he was still with the disciples at the end. In both cases, the call comes completely as a divine initiative to people who are ready to accept God's intervention in their lives although they are not actively seeking it. Samuel in his bed and Nathanael under his fig tree offer us portraits of ordinary life. Jesus elsewhere affirms this tendency for the divine to interrupt the routine, for the salvation or judgment of God to manifest itself when and where it is least expected (Matt. 24:37-44). As we have noted, this accent on God's initiative is to be stressed over the character or qualities of the persons called. Neither Samuel nor Nathanael are described as especially gifted; their primary virtue is basic human integrity, which is manifested in willingness to hear (1 Sam. 3:10) or see (John 1:46) what God is doing. They are people who, paradoxically, are prepared to be surprised.

Although God's initiative is highlighted, both accounts of the divine call also employ human agency. The extra characters of Eli and Philip seem unnecessary in one sense. Either call narrative could easily have been related without mention of these characters, but neither is, and this may itself be significant. In the stories as we have them, Samuel would not have recognized the voice he heard as that of God apart from the perception of Eli (1 Sam. 3:8) and Nathanael would not have considered the possibility of anything good coming out of Nazareth apart from the invitation of Philip (John 1:45-46). Perhaps because the call comes in ways that are unexpected, its reception require assistance.

Third Sunday after the Epiphany
Third Sunday in Ordinary Time

Lectionary	First Lesson	Psalm	Second Lesson	Gospel
Revised Common	Jonah 3:1-5, 10	Ps. 62:5-12	1 Cor. 7:29-31	Mark 1:14-20
Episcopal (BCP)	Jer. 3:21—4:2	Psalm 130	1 Cor. 7:17-23	Mark 1:14-20
Roman Catholic	Jonah 3:1-5, 10	Ps. 25:4-9	1 Cor. 7:29-31	Mark 1:14-20
Lutheran (LBW)	Jonah 3:1-5, 10	Ps. 62:6-14	1 Cor. 7:29-31	Mark 1:14-20

FIRST LESSON: JONAH 3:1-5, 10

The book of Jonah is a humorous folktale, the point and humor of which are often missed. For example, the city of Nineveh is described in 3:3 as "a large city even for God," an expression that is intended to bring a chuckle but seldom does because most English translations rephrase the passage (NRSV: "exceedingly large") to avoid offending literalists—even though this means depriving the rest of us! Similarly, we might ask why lectionary committees have omitted vv. 6-9 from today's lesson. Perhaps, they feared the description of repentance here would sound ridiculous. But that is the whole point—it is supposed to be ridiculous. No one would really dress their cattle in sackcloth and make their animals go forty days without food or water to be sure they were as penitent as their owners. For that matter, to the original readers of this tale, the image of the great Assyrian king dressed in sackcloth would have seemed as ridiculous as that of the farm animals. A modern comparison would be a story that related how, at the voice of a single Jewish child, the entire Nazi empire from Hitler on down was transformed into a company of saints. The readers are expected to know this didn't really happen. It is a joke. They are expected to laugh.

The basic joke underlying the entire story lies in its satirical depiction of Jonah as the reluctant prophet. This is portrayed not only in the hilarious fish episode of the first two chapters but also in the text for today. Having discovered he cannot escape God completely, Jonah now does as he is told, albeit as half-heartedly as possible. He only "begins to go into the city" and his oracle is a one-liner, delivered without enthusiasm or style (v. 4). This portrait goes against type for prophets, who were thought to be nothing if they were not flowery and impassioned. But, as the story continues, what other prophets hoped for in vain with years of preaching and tremendous oracles is now accomplished with a single sentence by a prophet who didn't even want to succeed. Every single individual in the greatest and most evil city on earth repents and puts his or her faith in God.

At this point, the joke works on several levels. First, the success reported here may be at the expense of the prophetic profession, as if to indicate that prophets might do better if they'd just say their piece and be done with it. Second, this depiction lampoons the current spiritual status of Israel, where most had adopted a minimalist expectation that hoped, at best, for a remnant of the people to be faithful. And finally, the tale ridicules the vindictive perspective that prefers to see enemies destroyed rather than converted. The real punch line comes in 4:2, where we learn the reason for Jonah's reluctance. It wasn't that he was lazy or feared persecution. It was because he knew God was gracious and merciful and thought that, if he were successful, Nineveh might be spared! Imagine the Jewish child in the analogous tale suggested above saying, "I didn't want Hitler to repent, because then he wouldn't go to hell where he belongs!"

We should note that the twofold response of the Ninevites is precisely that demanded by Jesus in our Gospel lesson for today (Mark 1:15). They "believed God" (v. 5) and "repented" (v. 10; NRSV "turned"). The first expression does not mean simply that they believed the message Jonah spoke (for then they would have despaired) but that they trusted in God and placed their lives utterly into God's hands (see 3:9). The second expression does not mean simply that they acknowledged or regretted their sins, but that they changed, turning from their evil ways and, specifically, from violence (3:8).

The thought of God changing God's mind (v. 10) may seem strange to some, though this has strong biblical precedent (Exod. 32:14). Actually, the scenario that is played out here is precisely that which is described hypothetically in Jer. 18:7-8. God's sovereignty always allows God to reserve the option to change plans. God is not bound by anything, not even (as careless theologians may say) by God's own word or promises. In the Bible, God can and often does act in ways that contradict what God previously announced, but there is not a single incidence of divine fluctuation working to the detriment of humanity. Rather, God's second thoughts always seem to be ones of greater leniency, grace, or mercy, as Jonah is depicted as knowing only too well (4:2).

SECOND LESSON: I CORINTHIANS 7:29-31

This passage is a self-contained rhetorical unit. Paul states a premise (v. 29a), explicates its implications (vv. 29b-31a), and then restates the premise (31b).

The premise is that the appointed time (*kairos*) has been shortened (NRSV, "grown short"), which means the essence (NRSV, "form") of this present world is passing away. By this, Paul does not necessarily mean that the parousia is going to occur soon (though he probably does believe this) or that the world as we know it is about to come to an end. Rather, Paul is combating a notion about the futility or capriciousness of life, a notion that is still with us today. In its most extreme form, this notion was expressed as a denial that history was moving toward any sort of goal and that events merely transpired randomly without meaning or purpose. As a Hebrew, Paul would have responded to this popular Greek concept by insisting that God created time (and, therefore, history) and would ultimately bring things to their appropriate conclusion (see the comments on Gen. 1:1-5 in last week's lessons). In a less extreme form, people could acknowledge God's intentions for the end of time while disregarding these as having much impact on their lives in the present world. This, of course, approximates the teaching of Deism, which had a vast influence on popular religion in America. God got everything started and God will someday bring everything to a close, but in the meantime, God pretty much expects us to take care of ourselves.

Against this notion, Paul asserts that God not only created time but now, through Jesus Christ, has effectively shortened time. The image characterizes time qualitatively as well as quantitatively. "Shortened time" is time moving toward consummation. How long time takes to reach its consummation is of little concern. What is important is that we now live in the time during which the process of God's purposes being fulfilled is underway. Because of what God has begun in Jesus, the future matters more now than ever before.

In spelling out the implications of this premise, Paul cites five instances of daily life: marriage, mourning, rejoicing, buying, and selling (dealing with the world). The latter four form pairs. Paul asserts that such activities ought to be transformed by the recognition of what God has done in Christ. The recitation here is rhetorical and could easily be misunderstood. Paul does not *literally* believe that people who have wives should live as though they have none, as he has made clear earlier in this chapter (vv. 3-5, 10-11). Nor does he believe that people should refrain from mourning or rejoicing (Rom. 12:15) or from engaging in commerce (2 Thess. 3:6-13). The point of his rhetoric is that God's action in Jesus Christ gives all of life a meaning and purpose that it does not otherwise seem to have. The purpose of marriage is not simply to be married, nor is the purpose of business just to make a living. Work and family, things that make us happy and things that make us sad—all these aspects of our existence in this present world now have eternal value that transcends and subverts the worth they appear to have in a world that is passing away.

GOSPEL: MARK 1:14-20

Biblical theologians often attach significance to pairs of indicative and imperative statements that identify, respectively, the activity of God and the expected activity of humanity. The distinction is comparable in some respects to Luther's hermeneutic of law and gospel, though it avoids the problematic semantics of defining law as something other than gospel while also insisting that it is a good gift of God (if the law is good, then isn't it "good news" = gospel?).

The Gospel lesson for today contains two pairs of indicative-imperative statements. In the first (v. 15), Jesus states that God's rule is imminent (indicative) and then demands that God's people respond to this announcement (imperative). The significance of the form is that, clearly, the imperative demand details the consequences of the indicative truth rather than vice-versa. The imminence of God's rule is in no way dependent upon human response, but the response described here (repentance and faith) is completely dependent upon the imminence of God's rule. Also significant is the observation that the entire proclamation of Jesus—both indicative and imperative statements—are described as "good news" (v. 14). This, then, is Mark's definition of "the gospel of God": God's rule is imminent, so imminent that repentance and faith are now possible and necessary.

The indicative statement in v. 15 contains two lines of synonymous parallelism (similar to 1 Cor. 7:29a and 31b in our second lesson). First, Jesus says that the appointed time (*kairos*) is fulfilled, and then he clarifies this by telling us which appointed time is fulfilled: the time for the coming of God's kingdom. The English word *fulfilled* may be misleading if it carries a connotation of completion. The point is that the decisive moment has arrived, but not that it is over. Rather, we are in it. Similarly, the Greek word *ēggiken* (NRSV, "come near") is ambiguous for it can mean either "already here" or "soon to arrive." This ambiguity is intentional and should not be resolved, for a major point in the Synoptic Gospels is that we live in eschatological tension between the "already" and the "not yet." Thus, Jesus can instruct his followers to pray for God's kingdom to come in one instance (Matt. 6:10) and then insist that God's kingdom has already come in another (Matt. 12:28). To resolve this ambiguity on the side of the "already" can lead to a naive or presumptuous theology of glory; to resolve it on the side of the "not yet" can lead to a humanistic existentialism that fails to recognize the present activity of God or to an otherworldly pietism that defers benefits of the gospel to life beyond death. We may think of the coming of God's kingdom as the accomplishment of God's will, for God can only truly be said to rule when what God wants to happen takes place. Thus, the Synoptic Gospels want to affirm the good news that God's will is being done, here and now, while also recognizing that what sometimes happens here and now is not the will of God.

The imperative statement in v. 15 also consists of two lines of synonymous parallelism. "Repent" and "believe in the good news" do not represent two appropriate responses to the gospel Jesus proclaims but two different ways of describing the only appropriate response. Faith is neither the cause nor the consequence of repentance but its substance. If the time of God's rule is in fact arriving, this calls for a radically new way of thinking and acting. In this context, to repent means to believe the good news that God's rule is at hand, which in turn means to reorient oneself in such a way that everything will now be affected by awareness of this truth.

A second pair of indicative-imperative statements occurs in the episode that follows this proclamation. Jesus calls disciples, saying "Follow me!" (imperative) and "I will make you fish for people" (indicative). This time, however, the imperative comes first and the promise expressed in the indicative is conditional. God's rule remains imminent whether we repent and believe or not, but Jesus makes us fish for people only if we follow him. The emphasis in the imperative demand is on the proper subordinate relationship of the disciple to Jesus. In Mark's Gospel, people fail to follow Jesus either by rejecting his call altogether (10:21-22) or by accepting the call and then trying to subvert the master-disciple relationship. The same words Jesus speaks to Peter here (*opisō mou*) are repeated to Peter later in what we usually read as "Get behind me (*opisō mou*), Satan" (8:33). When Peter forgets his station and rebukes Jesus (8:32), Jesus reminds him that his role is not to lead but to follow. Following Jesus means staying behind him, not getting ahead of him.

Those who do follow Jesus are enabled to "fish for people." They do this, as Jesus did, by announcing good news. In fact, those who follow Jesus will proclaim the gospel to all nations (13:10). The gospel they preach, however, is not just the "gospel of God" brought by Jesus (1:14) but also "the gospel of Jesus Christ, the Son of God" (1:1). This includes not only the general message of God's imminent reign but also the specific message of how God's will has been accomplished through the life, death, and resurrection of Jesus.

CONNECTIONS

The connections between the three lessons for today are unusually close. Certainly, the similarities between Paul's declaration in 1 Cor. 7:29-32 and Jesus' announcement in Mark 1:14-15 far outweigh any differences we might detect. Paul says the *kairos* ("appointed time") has been shortened, while Jesus says it is being fulfilled. Both mean to indicate that the long-awaited era of consummation has begun and is currently underway. Paul would probably date the inception of this new age to the resurrection of Christ, while the Gospel of Mark links it to Jesus' baptism (Mark 1:9-11), but both believe the eternal reign of God is being established such that the essence of the world as we know it is passing away. Both believe that acknowledgment of this state of affairs calls for a radical reorientation, according to which all commitments are transformed and relativized. Both cite, specifically, commitments to work (Mark 1:18; 1 Cor. 7:30-31) and family (Mark 1:20; 1 Cor. 7:29) as examples of such reorientation.

Both the Gospel reading and the first lesson choose the same names for this reorientation of life. It may be called either "believing" (Mark 1:15; Jonah 3:5) or "repentance" (Mark 1:15; Jonah 3:10). When these two lessons are compared, what is most surprising is that in Jonah the message that calls forth this response is apparently a pronouncement of pure doom (3:4) while in Mark it is an announcement of "good news" (1:14). Luther would see this as an instance of God working to our benefit through either law or gospel. Or, we might say that God's will is always for the benefit of humanity, but whether individuals perceive that will as threat or promise depends on the position they occupy with regard to it. Since God's will is to establish justice in all the earth, this posed an initial threat to the Ninevites since it meant their unjust city would be overthrown (3:4). But once they turned from evil and violence, the accomplishment of God's will was no longer a threat. God changed God's mind but God's will did not change. The transformation of the Ninevites allowed God to revise the plan for how the divine will for justice could be implemented.

In a similar way, the announcement of Jesus might not be considered "good news" by those who do not want to see God's rule established—by those who, for example, are currently first and discover that this means they will now be last (Mark 10:31). Thus, the same message may be perceived as threat and promise, law and gospel. To believe that God's kingdom has drawn near is to believe that God is interested in ruling our lives. This is (or should be) threatening, but ultimately it is good news because as Jesus' subsequent ministry and passion demonstrate, God's rule operates to defeat what is evil and to bring about what is good. All who orient their lives to God in trust will find the initially threatening announcement that God's will is going to be done transformed into a promise.

Fourth Sunday after the Epiphany
Fourth Sunday in Ordinary Time

Lectionary	First Lesson	Psalm	Second Lesson	Gospel
Revised Common	Deut. 18:15-20	Psalm 111	1 Cor. 8:1-13	Mark 1:21-28
Episcopal (BCP)	Deut. 18:15-20	Psalm 111	1 Cor. 8:1b-13	Mark 1:21-28
Roman Catholic	Deut. 18:15-20	Ps. 95:1-2, 6-9	1 Cor. 7:32-35	Mark 1:21-28
Lutheran (LBW)	Deut. 18:15-20	Psalm 1	1 Cor. 8:1-13	Mark 1:21-28

FIRST LESSON: DEUTERONOMY 18:15-20

This passage can be read on two levels: pragmatic and eschatological. The latter is canonical, but the former provides the interpretation closest to that intended for the original context. We will start there.

The book of Deuteronomy took shape during the seventh century B.C.E. as part of the reform movements attributed to Josiah. A major impetus of these reforms was the elimination of syncretistic religious practices. Such practices had become widespread for a variety of reasons, but one major cause was the simple reality that people seeking divine guidance were willing to accept help wherever they thought they could get it. Soothsayers, diviners, sorcerers, and the like had become popular. Some of these were no doubt sincere practitioners, while others were probably just con artists, but in any case their claims to be able to discern and influence the powers of the spiritual realm were considered deceptive and dangerous by the Deuteronomistic reform movement (see the verses immediately preceding our text, Deut. 18:9-14).

As an alternative to reliance on occult arts, Deuteronomy promises that the Lord will raise up prophets like Moses for the people. (Even if the word *prophet* in vv. 15 and 18 is singular—and there is some dispute about this—the verb "raise up" is distributive and means, "From time to time, I will raise up . . ."). The promise is placed on the lips of Moses himself, as the book recalls his final address to the people several centuries earlier. As if to answer the question, "Why can't everyone just decide for him or herself?" the text refers to an event reported earlier in Deuteronomy 5. According to that narrative, all the people did gather at Mt. Horeb to hear the law, but after the Ten Commandments were given, they found the experience to be so overwhelming that they begged Moses to become their mediator. Thus, they were able to return to their tents (and to their daily lives) while Moses listened to the voice of God and passed on what God had said. In Deuteronomy 5, Moses recalled this story to explain his unique position; now, in Deuteronomy 18, he indicates that this was a precedent for how God would work in the future.

On a pragmatic level, then, this text offers a way for people to receive divine guidance within the accepted channels of religion. The system will only work if the people are loyal to the prophets and the prophets are loyal to the Lord, but the approach our lesson takes to encouraging such loyalty is interesting. A prophet who misrepresents the Lord is to be put to death (v. 20), but people who disobey a prophet are not to be punished (v. 19). God will of course ultimately hold all people accountable, but within the sphere of human activity, the greater onus of responsibility is clearly on the prophet, not the people. This raises the question of criteria for determining the true prophet from the false. Verse 20 returns to the notion of syncretism, identifying false prophets as those who either openly or deceptively present ideas that are associated with other gods. Verses 21-22 continue this thought by identifying false prophets as those who make predictions that do not come true, but this would not be helpful for prophecy that is not explicitly predictive (for example, that which offers ethical counsel). The best criterion is probably to be found in the description of God's prophets as being "like Moses." As Von Rad notes in his commentary on *Deuteronomy* (Philadelphia: Westminster Press, 1966), Moses is portrayed throughout Deuteronomy as a figure who intercedes, suffers, and even dies on behalf of the people (4:21-22; 9:18-20, 25-29). If Moses is the prototype for prophets, the true prophet will be marked by a spirit of service and sacrifice, as one who cares more for the people than for his or her own welfare (Von Rad, 124).

That this pragmatic level of interpretation was not entirely satisfying can be seen from the conclusion of the book of Deuteronomy, where we read, "Never since has there arisen a prophet in Israel like Moses" (34:10). Even the compilers of this book sensed that the promise of such prophets had never really been fulfilled, and so the text came quickly to be read in an eschatological way. Now, the promise was interpreted as being that at some time, God would send a single great prophet, a second Moses, who would be their mediator. This text was given a messianic interpretation at Qumran and in the New Testament. In the latter, of course, it is seen to be fulfilled in Jesus. Several passages in the Gospel of John (1:21-45; 6:14; 7:40) allude to this identification, as do speeches in the book of Acts (3:22-23; 7:37).

SECOND LESSON: I CORINTHIANS 8:1-13

The issue of eating food offered to idols appears to have been a big controversy in the first-century church, for Paul deals with it at length both in Romans 14 and 1 Cor. 8:1—11:1. The controversy itself is no longer with us, but Paul's treatment of it remains relevant as an example of conflict resolution and as a paradigm for ethics.

The issue appears to have been twofold: Some Christians bought and ate meat in the marketplace which, according to common practice, came from an animal that had been slaughtered as a sacrifice to the Roman gods. Also, some Christians (probably the same ones) attended meals held at pagan temples which, though officially worship events, were also grand social occasions and an important source of business contacts. The text for today introduces a discussion of both these issues, but the emphasis here appears to be on the latter (v. 10).

The argument these Corinthians have put forward is that eating "idol food" is idolatry only if one believes the idol or false god truly exists. Since they know that "there is no God but one" (v. 4), they can attend the temple banquets and eat the food dedicated to idols without it affecting them one way or the other (v. 8). Eventually, Paul will disagree with them on this point (10:14-22). Paul believes the gods of these temples are demons, real spiritual beings, not nonexistent entities. Partaking in the temple banquets involves a partnership with demons that may have consequences analogous to those associated with sharing in the body and blood of Christ in the eucharist (see also 11:23-32).

But none of this is found in the verses selected for today. Here, Paul appears to accept their argument, such as it is, and focuses on what is for him an even more important point. The essential criterion for determining Christian conduct is not knowledge, but love (vv. 1-3).

The question posed by Christian ethics is not, "What do I have a right to do?" but "What can I do that will be most helpful to others?" Thus, even if an action is not wrong in and of itself, it becomes sin (v. 12) if it is a stumbling block to others (v. 9). The eating of idol food on the part of knowledgeable Christians may lead less knowledgeable, weak Christians (v. 7) to become involved in idolatry at such a level that they are in fact "destroyed" (vv. 10-11).

Concern for others is the bottom line for Paul. Here, he chooses to articulate the principle of exercising concern for others as his main argument against partaking in temple banquets, although he could have condemned this practice on other grounds (10:14-22). Later, he will invoke this same principle to commend discernment in knowing when to eat food from the marketplace, even though he finds this practice to be otherwise acceptable (10:23-28). In fact, as he says in the concluding verse of today's lesson, he would be willing to give up eating meat altogether if this were necessary to keep others from falling. The enunciation of this principle is what will lead Paul eventually to the great hymn of love later in this letter, which says, "If I have . . . all knowledge . . . but do not have love, I am nothing" (1 Cor. 13:2).

GOSPEL: MARK 1:21-28

This pericope demonstrates well the distinction form critics and redaction critics make between "tradition" and "framework." Units of material that were passed on through oral transmission followed typical patterns that helped to facilitate memory. The typical outline for an exorcism story had four parts: (1) the demon recognizes the exorcist; (2) the exorcist rebukes the demon; (3) the demon comes out, making an impression; and, (4) the effect on the spectators is noted. A glance at today's text reveals that vv. 23-27a fit this outline perfectly. Thus, scholars often believe that Mark received this part of the story through oral tradition and then added vv. 21-22 and 27b-28 (the "framework") when he fit the unit into his Gospel.

We cannot be sure that this analysis of the compositional process is correct, but the distinction between what appears to be the traditional core and the somewhat unique introduction and conclusion is helpful nonetheless. Within the context of Mark's Gospel, 1:23-27a would be meaningful even without this framework, for it provides an actualization of the claim Jesus announced in our Gospel lesson last week, namely that the reign of God is imminent (1:14-15). Demons in the New Testament are a cause of disease and disability. They prevent people's lives from being what God wants them to be. As this text shows, the rule of demons has extended into the sphere of the sacred, such that people may be subject to their attack even in a synagogue on a sabbath. But now Jesus backs up his claim that *God's* rule has come near by ending this antithetical rule of demons. We witness what Markan scholar David Rhoads likes to call "a local skirmish in the cosmic struggle." If Jesus is plundering the devil's house, then someone must have bound the devil (3:27).

The event does not prove Jesus is God's agent (3:22), but for those who recognize that he is God's agent, it reveals what God's rule is like. God's rule liberates from oppression and banishes all that is evil (sin, disease, death). It is a rule of grace: the man does not exhibit any qualities to commend his healing, not even faith. Jesus has come to announce and enact

God's rule on earth and he does this by authoritatively putting into effect the will of God, which is marked by compassion, healing, and mercy.

Now let us consider the framework that Mark provides for this already meaningful text. Why does he introduce and conclude the story with twin references to the authoritative teaching of Jesus? Mark probably does this to give new relevance to the historical remembrance of how Jesus used to cast demons out of people when he walked the earth years ago. In one sense, Jesus the exorcist is no longer present (see 2:20; 14:7), but his teaching is still with the community. The framework for the text transforms it from a simple exorcism story into a testimony to the authoritative word of Jesus. The point is that this authoritative word, contained in the teaching of Jesus, carries the same liberating power that was evident in the person of Jesus. Through its proclamation of Jesus' word and faithfulness to his teaching, the church continues to enact God's rule and banish the demonic.

CONNECTIONS

A common theme in all three lessons for today is the exercise of authority. In Deut. 18:15-20 we are told that God will provide people with the divine guidance they seek. The role of the prophet is one of tremendous authority, but the character of God's prophet justifies such authority. The true prophet of God will be "like Moses," a person whose authority is exercised through service.

The theme of authority may be less apparent in the second lesson, but the word the NRSV translates "liberty" in 1 Cor. 8:9 is *exousia*—exactly the same word rendered as "authority" in Mark 1:22, 27. This indicates that the dispute over idol food in Corinth has gone well beyond academic debate to become a power struggle. The liberty that some of the Corinthians claim is in fact authority to determine their own lives without consideration of others. This, Paul argues, is not a Christian concept of authority.

In the Gospel lesson Jesus demonstrates divine authority through performing an act of kindness that liberates an oppressed person from demonic tyranny. After reading the Gospel text for last week (Mark 1:14-20), we might have expected Jesus and his followers to start enacting the rule of God by making people do the things that God requires. This doesn't happen. In fact, Jesus never once uses his divine powers to make anybody do anything. God's rule is not coercive as is the rule of demons. Instead, the rule of God is manifested as Jesus exercises authority in service to others, through teaching and healing. In this way, Jesus demonstrates what he will later say to his disciples about authority: it is not for lording over others, but for serving them, even as he came not to be served but to serve (10:42-45).

Fifth Sunday after the Epiphany
Fifth Sunday in Ordinary Time

Lectionary	First Lesson	Psalm	Second Lesson	Gospel
Revised Common	Isa. 40:21-31	Ps. 147:1-11, 20c	1 Cor. 9:16-23	Mark 1:29-39
Episcopal (BCP)	2 Kings 4:(8-17)18-21, (22-31) 32-37	Psalm 142	1 Cor. 9:16-23	Mark 1:29-39
Roman Catholic	Job 7:1-4, 6-7	Ps. 147:1-6	1 Cor. 9:16-19, 22-23	Mark 1:29-39
Lutheran (LBW)	Job 7:1-7	Ps. 147:1-13	1 Cor. 9:16-23	Mark 1:29-39

FIRST LESSON: ISAIAH 40:21-31

This poetic oracle, ascribed to Second Isaiah, is addressed to Israel during the time of the Babylonian exile. During this exceptionally difficult time, God's people experienced humiliation and oppression such as they had not known for centuries. As v. 27 reveals, they began to question whether they could rely on God to help them.

The purpose of the oracle is to offer comfort (40:1) and inspire trust—in a word, to create hope. The means for accomplishing this is itself significant. Rather than offering a new word, the prophet summons people to recall tradition, to remember what they have been told from the beginning (v. 21). The oracle also facilitates this by quoting familiar phrases from liturgy in vv. 22-24, 26, and 28.

The complaints voiced by Israel in v. 27 highlight two concerns for the prophet to address. The first complaint, "My way is hidden from the LORD," implies that God does not know of Israel's plight and so is not able to help. The second complaint, "My right is disregarded by my God," implies that God is not concerned with justice for Israel and so does not care to help.

The prophet affirms both God's power and inclination to save. Recognizing God as Creator serves to bolster confidence in the former, for the one who created the heavens and the earth is able to control what happens therein. To the Creator, all inhabitants of the earth are "like grasshoppers" (v. 22), including supposedly mighty rulers (v. 23). The Creator is everlasting (v. 28), whereas rulers and their empires are as transient as a plant that springs up and then withers (v. 24; compare 40:6-8). Even the stars, which in Babylon were regarded as deities, are but created things controlled by the Lord who is "great in strength, mighty in power."

God's concern for Israel is assured through recall of another traditional tenet—not, as we might expect, the covenant with Abraham or Moses or David, but rather what has come to be known today as God's "preferential option for the poor." Israel can know that God will help because God "gives power to the faint and strengthens the powerless" (v. 29). If God's people remember their tradition, then the status of oppression that they currently experience will itself become a source of hope, for in the tradition God's concern is consistently directed to the disadvantaged.

The oracle is misinterpreted when read as a rebuke of Israel's complaint, bemoaning the people's lack of faith or challenging the view that freedom is a "right" rather than a gift or privilege (v. 27). Although these observations have some theological validity, the language of v. 27 is traditional for lament (compare Pss. 13:1; 35:23; 44:24; 88:14) and within Scripture such language is acceptable to God. In other words, God does not scrutinize the cries of the oppressed to determine whether they are theologically adequate; nor does the prophet here condemn Israel for feeling helpless. The point, rather, is to offer a vision of hope that will cut through this desperation and enable Israel to rise above it.

Interpretation also takes a wrong turn when the final verse (v. 31) is taken to extol the virtue of passivity. No contrast is intended between ones who wait (passively) for the Lord and others who work (actively) to improve their situation. The people encouraged to wait for the Lord are "powerless" (v. 29): working to improve their situation does not appear to be an option, much less a temptation. The phrase "wait for the LORD" (which can also be translated "hope in the LORD") describes an active orientation that produces renewal of strength. The concluding lines of v. 31 do not describe future benefits that will eventually come to those who wait for the Lord but present experiences of those who currently are waiting for the Lord. Even in the midst of oppression, they are able to "mount up with wings like eagles," "run and not be weary," "walk and not faint."

SECOND LESSON: I CORINTHIANS 9:16-23

The main point of this important section of Paul's letter concerns the voluntary relinquishment of rights for the sake of others. Christians are free, but for Christians freedom is not an end in itself. Rather, it is a means to a greater end: meeting the needs of others. Thus the paradox, "free to serve," which Paul also explicates in Galatians 5.

The verses here are autobiographical, but Paul believes others should be willing to make similar sacrifices (see 1 Cor. 11:1). When he calls upon the

Corinthians to relinquish their rights for the sake of others, Paul wants them to know he is not asking them to do anything that he does not do himself. He chooses two examples: working without financial remuneration (vv. 16-18) and adopting the social customs of those to whom he ministers (vv. 19-23). In the verses preceding today's lesson, Paul gave several reasons why he would have had a right to be paid for his ministry among the Corinthians (9:4-14). Other apostles—even oxen!—have a rightful claim to benefit from their labor. Still, Paul and Barnabas worked to support themselves (9:6, compare 1 Thess. 2:9), probably in Aquila and Priscilla's tentmaking shop (Acts 18:1-3), in order to proclaim the gospel free of charge (9:18). Just being able to do this was reward enough for Paul, for the gospel he preaches concerns the free gift of God's salvation (Rom. 6:23) and the opportunity to proclaim this without cost allows him to demonstrate grace even as he announces it (compare Matt. 10:8).

In delineating these points, Paul describes a double irony. His understanding of his call to ministry seems close to that of slavery: an obligation has been laid upon him that he must fulfill regardless of whether it brings a reward or accords with his own will (vv. 16-17). But—the first irony—being Christ's slave makes him free with respect to all others (v. 19a). In one sense, this was fulfilled literally in Corinth. Since he did not receive pay, he did not become beholden to anyone. But—the second irony—even though he was under no obligation to anyone, he chose to behave as though he were a slave to everyone (v. 19b). In all of their encounters, he deferred to their ways rather than expecting them to defer to his. He moved back and forth from Greco-Roman households to "kosher" Jewish homes, adopting the manners and customs appropriate to each (vv. 19-22).

We should not regard Paul's practice of becoming "all things to all people" (v. 22) as a sign of vacillation on his part. Paul is anything but wishy-washy; he is absolutely intransigent on matters that he considers essential (1 Cor. 1:22-23; 5:1-5). But neither should we assume that he is being accommodating on matters that are of no importance to him, for that would deny any element of personal sacrifice. The point is that "for the sake of the gospel" Paul is willing to forego his own preferences and inclinations (compare 8:13).

The context for the passage suggests two immediate areas of application. The first is conflict resolution. The Corinthian congregation is divided over many issues and a root cause for some of their problems is the insistence of some members on getting their rights even at the expense of others. (In this regard, see last week's lesson [8:1-13; compare 10:23-28].) The second area of application is cross-cultural evangelism. Paul recognizes the necessity of transcending cultural boundaries if he is to "win" people for Christ (the phrase is repeated five times in vv. 19-22). He accepts this inconvenience so that he might share in the gospel's blessings (v. 23) which, of course, include participation in a community inclusive of all nations.

GOSPEL: MARK 1:29-39

Taken together with last week's lesson, this text presents Mark's picture of a typical day in the life of Jesus. Jesus attends the synagogue and casts a demon out of a man (1:21-28). Then, he goes with his disciples to Peter's house, where he heals Peter's mother-in-law. Later that evening, the whole city gathers to the door and he heals many people and drives out many demons. After this we might expect him to be tired, but he rises early and goes off alone to pray. His devotions are interrupted by the news that everyone is looking for him and, as a new day begins, he sets out to minister in a similar way elsewhere.

The story of Peter's mother-in-law (vv. 29-31) has some interesting features. This is the only incident ever reported concerning her (compare Matt. 8:14-15; Luke 4:38-39), and Peter's wife is never mentioned in the Gospels, though Paul says she later accompanied Peter in his missionary travels (1 Cor. 9:5). Most unusual is the mention that after the healing, she "began to serve them" (v. 31). Although in a literal sense this may just mean that she prepared a meal, the Greek word for "serve" (*diakoneō*) is the same word used in early Christianity for deacons and ministers of the church (Acts 6:1-6; compare Romans 16:1; Phil. 1:1; 1 Tim. 3:8-13). Healing stories rarely mention such responsive activity on the part of the one healed, but Mark's Gospel seems to emphasize presentations of women who act in a way that is commendable (7:24-30; 12:41-44; 14:3-9; 15:40-41; 16:1).

In the description of multiple healings that evening (vv. 32-34), Mark notes that Jesus "would not permit the demons to speak, because they knew him" (v. 34). The silencing of demons is also a recurrent theme in this Gospel (compare 1:25, 34; 3:12). This may reflect a power struggle, according to which the demons attempt to gain control of the exorcist by naming him or her (and vice-versa—see Mark 5:9). In addition, Mark clearly does not want the mystery of Christ's identity to be revealed to the world by demons. Ultimately, this mystery can only be revealed by God through the cross (15:39) and resurrection (9:9), which is why Jesus not only silences demons but commands secrecy among humans (1:44; 5:43; 7:36; 9:9).

Peter seems already to have forgotten that his call is to *follow* Jesus (1:16-17) rather than to become his manager (vv. 35-37). When the text says that he and his companions "hunted for" (*katadiōkō*) Jesus, the word used is one that the Bible usually translates as "persecute." Their words, "Everyone is searching for you" imply a rebuke (compare 8:32). These disciples are enamored of the public acclaim Jesus is receiving and they can't understand why he would miss it to pray (compare 6:46; 14:32). Here is an early indication that they are setting their minds "not on divine things but on human things" (8:33). Already, we may note that Peter's attitude offers a remarkable contrast to that of his mother-in-law, who serves.

In v. 38, Jesus explicitly states why he has come (see also 2:17; 10:45; compare Matt. 5:17; Luke 19:10; John 10:10). His mission is "to proclaim the message," namely the gospel message of God's reign articulated in 1:15. Calvin thought this verse established the superiority of preaching over miracles, which are but "appendages to the Word." This is unlikely. In Capernaum, Jesus proclaimed the message in word and deed, teaching with authority and performing saving acts that demonstrated the nature and reality of God's rule (1:21-27). The point of v. 38 is not that he determines to preach elsewhere, avoiding a crowd that wants more miracles. Rather, since his work here is done, he determines to continue proclaiming the message through word and deed elsewhere (v. 39) instead of just hanging around to absorb accolades.

This passage presents God's rule as *power* (compare 14:62). This power overcomes both demons and disease and it operates in homes as surely as in synagogues. God's healing power is personal, affecting individuals, but it is available to all. It renews the lives of women and men. In short, as the kingdom of God draws near (1:15), God's healing power comes to all sorts of people in all sorts of places with all sorts of problems.

CONNECTIONS

The clearest connection between the texts for this day is found in the affirmation of the compassionate power of God sounded in the first lesson and the Gospel. Isaiah emphasizes the power of God as Creator over the cosmos and, therefore, over the petty rulers of the earth. Mark highlights the power of God's rule manifest in Jesus to overcome demons and disease. If we wish to distinguish further, we might say the problem addressed in the first lesson is the oppression of people as a nation or a community, while in the Gospel it is the affliction of people as individuals. Or, we might typify the power of God in Isaiah as challenging political (and therefore, socioeconomic) oppression that comes upon people from without and the power of God in Mark as overcoming spiritual maladies that afflict people from within.

Such distinctions, however, can go too far. As Isa. 40:27 indicates, the problem of political oppression has caused spiritual distress. What the people need most is revival of hope and renewal of strength. Also, as Jesus goes about plundering the house of Satan in Mark's Gospel (3:27), ostensibly healing individuals of spiritual trauma, he is effectively creating a new social order. The establishment of God's rule is destroying all bases for purity codes that stratify society and relegate the sick and the afflicted to the bottom of the scale. We do well, therefore, to take these two lessons together as expressing God's will for wholeness in human beings and in human society.

A connection may also be noted between Mark 1:38 and 1 Cor. 9:16. Just as Jesus identifies proclaiming the gospel message as the thing that he has come to do, so Paul interprets his call to proclaim the gospel as a sacred commission and he does all for the sake of it (1 Cor. 9:23). Indeed, Paul's Christlike attitude displayed throughout our second lesson serves as one more testimony to the transforming effects of God's compassionate power. Neither politically oppressed nor demon-possessed, Paul represents one who has been freed from self-service and prejudice to live in commitment to others.

Sixth Sunday after the Epiphany
Sixth Sunday in Ordinary Time
Proper 1

Lectionary	First Lesson	Psalm	Second Lesson	Gospel
Revised Common	2 Kings 5:1-14	Psalm 30	I Cor. 9:24-27	Mark 1:40-45
Episcopal (BCP)	2 Kings 5:1-15b	Ps. 42 *or* 42:1-7	I Cor. 9:24-27	Mark 1:40-45
Roman Catholic	Lev. 13:1-2, 44-46	Ps. 32:1-2, 5, 7, 11	I Cor. 10:31—11:1	Mark 1:40-45
Lutheran (LBW)	2 Kings 5:1-14	Psalm 32	I Cor. 9:24-27	Mark 1:40-45

FIRST LESSON: 2 KINGS 5:1-14

Best known perhaps as the successor to Elijah, Elisha the "man of God" (v. 8) was a prophet in Israel during the ninth century B.C.E. Like his forebear, he is remembered more for his miracles than his oracles, which means only that the mode of proclamation differs from that of the later "writing prophets." Recounted now as part of the Deuteronomistic history, the deeds of Elisha witness primarily to the saving power of God, though sometimes the message is one of judgment also (see the conclusion to the present story in 5:20-27).

A few commentators understand this account of Naaman's healing as a nationalistic tale designed to prove the superiority of Israel's faith over Syrian religion. But the story has a strong universal tendency that under-cuts such narrow interests. Notably, the king of Israel exhibits less faith than the Arameans (v. 7). Also, Naaman is introduced to us as a person by whom "the LORD had given victory to Aram" (v. 1). This amazing verse indicates that God has been with Naaman (and with the nation of Aram!) all along. Far from being nationalistic, the story intends to demonstrate that the God who has been revealed in Israel is in fact the God of all the earth (5:15). In Luke 4:27, Jesus cites this story as evidence against nation-alistic religion.

Although Naaman finds the healing he seeks, it does not come about in the way that he expects or for the reasons that he anticipates. In v. 11 we hear his disappointment that the prophet did not "wave his hand over the spot" or invoke the name of his God, actions that might bespeak a magical conception of healing. But there is more to it than this. In the Hebrew text of v. 11, the words "for me" are emphatic. Naaman complains that he is not being accorded the attention he thinks would be warranted: "I thought that *for me* he would surely come out."

This sense of personal importance, fueled by his own nationalistic pride (v. 12), prevents Naaman from recognizing his quest for healing as an appeal for mercy. He comes to Israel with the assumption that he will have to incur favor on the basis of his position, his royal letter of reference, and his lavish gifts. These count for nothing. When he arrives at Elisha's door with great pomp and circumstance, the prophet does not even bother to see him but sends a messenger with some simple instructions (vv. 9-10). Though Naaman is promised healing, he responds with indignation, offended at the thought that what he desires so greatly can be obtained so easily and that the offer apparently has nothing to do with his status. Ironically, he would have been more pleased if the prophet had commanded him to do some difficult task by which he could show that he had earned the right to be healed (v. 13). Luther was quick to identify Naaman's dilemma as a paradigm of works righteousness and, subsequently, to regard the bath in the Jordan as a type of Christian baptism. Modern scholarship may scoff at such uncritical interpretations but, in truth, they are not far off the mark. The text portrays God's gift of mercy as a scandal of grace, insofar as it reflects favorably upon the character of the giver rather than upon that of the recipient.

We also should not ignore the character of the Hebrew slave girl (v. 2), whose confident faith makes a sharp contrast to the despair of Israel's king (v. 7). For Naaman, the way to healing is a descent into humility that begins with heeding the message of this lowly slave girl and ends with immersion in foreign waters he considers inferior to those of his homeland. The detour that involves two royal courts, several bags of riches, and a few horses and chariots leads nowhere.

SECOND LESSON: I CORINTHIANS 9:24-27

Paul is writing to the city that invented gladiatorial combat. During his lifetime, the Isthmian games held there were as famous as the Olympics. Corinth sponsored these games every two years and we may surmise that the competition held in 51 C.E. when Paul was a resident made an impression beyond the probable commercial boost to his little tentmaking operation. Athletes were required under oath to enter a rigorous ten-month training program that included a strict diet and abstention from alcoholic beverages and sexual relations. All this in a city that was known for its relaxed moral standards.

Paul seizes on this metaphor to clarify the point that he has been discussing in our readings for the past three Sundays. Christians are free from the law but they are called to exercise this freedom advisedly, choosing behavior that is beneficial to themselves and to the community (6:12). As with most metaphors, the point may be lost if it is pushed too far. Although in a race "only one receives the prize" (v. 24), Paul does not mean to encourage competition among Christians or to imply that one wins only by beating out others. Or again, the point cannot be that the imperishable reward of eternal salvation can only be achieved through great effort, for this would contradict what Paul says elsewhere about justification by grace through faith. In that regard, Rom. 5:1-5 makes an interesting comparison to this text.

The main point is simply that, like athletes, Christians embrace discipline and self-control. For Christians, life has purpose, and decisions must therefore be made concerning what does or does not serve that purpose. Just as athletes forgo things that are not helpful for reaching their goal, so Christians give up behavior that would be out of place in the kingdom of God (6:9) or actions that have consequences that might prove harmful to others (8:7-13).

The concern here is self-restraint, not asceticism, but we should be careful not to tone down Paul's expectation to the extent that it is no longer challenging. In this epistle, he cites voluntary adoption of celibacy (7:25-35) or vegetarianism (8:13) as examples of the sort of lifestyle commitments one might feel called to make. We should also be careful about spiritualizing the message. Countless sermons on this text have encouraged Christians to prepare themselves spiritually (through prayer, devotion, fellowship, and the like) in the same way that athletes prepare themselves physically. Paul heartily endorses spiritual discipline, but this text is concerned specifically with the body (v. 27). Unlike Greeks (and Americans) who adopt a Platonic doctrine of the immortality of the soul, Paul believes the body itself is godly (6:19) and has a future with God (15:35-57). Therefore, we ought to glorify God in our bodies (6:20).

GOSPEL: MARK 1:40-45

Mark's story of Jesus healing a leper is charged with emotion. The leper begs for healing, kneeling before Jesus. Jesus is "moved with pity" and touches the leper. A textual variant in v. 41 describes Jesus as "becoming angry," a reading most translations reject but many commentators prefer. If the variant is accepted, the point is probably that Jesus is angry with the leprosy, which is personified (see v. 42), rather than with the leper. In any case, Jesus then becomes stern and warns the leper with instructions that appear to be ignored.

The narrative touches on several themes important to Mark's Gospel. It portrays well the Markan concept of faith as distinct from presumption. Confidence in divine power is faith but confidence in our own knowledge of the divine will is presumption. Mark's narrative repeatedly stresses the need for the former (5:36; 6:5-6; 9:23) while also insisting that no human being—not even Jesus—can fathom the will of God (10:40; 14:36). Thus, the apparent "blanket promises" associated with prayer (11:23-24) assume a bold confidence in God's power that is tempered by humble submission to God's will. The proper attitude is conveyed perfectly here in the words of the leper: "If you will, you can" (1:40).

The story emphasizes Jesus' compliance with the law in that he instructs the leper to do "what Moses commanded" (v. 44) even though this involves submission to the religious establishment that will prove hostile to Jesus. Jesus has already healed on the sabbath (1:21-28) and he will soon be challenged regarding practices that do not accord with the expectations of recognized legal experts (2:15-17, 18-20, 23-28; 3:1-6). As a preface to these conflicts, Mark wants to show that Jesus does respect the law of Moses. The conflicts come because the advent of God's rule announced by Jesus calls for reconsideration of how the law is to be interpreted and applied.

The story also illustrates Mark's concept of purity. The usual notion for the culture in which this Gospel was produced held that purity could only be maintained through separation from what was impure. Thus, God remained separate from humans in heaven or in a prescribed area of the temple (the "Holy of Holies") and people remained clean by avoiding contact with those who were unclean. Such a construal was defensive, granting to the impure the power to defile that which was pure. Mark's Gospel reverses this thinking, recognizing rather the power of that which is pure to cleanse the impure. Mark's concept is offensive (a pun, since it did and still does offend). Mark presents the coming of God's kingdom as an invasion of purity. The firmament (1:10) and the temple curtain (15:37) that separate God from humanity are torn asunder. When Jesus touches the leper (1:41), Jesus does not become unclean but the leper becomes clean.

Finally, much attention is focused on the command to silence that Jesus gives here (compare 5:43; 7:36; 8:26). Scholars often link these passages where Jesus enjoins silence regarding his miracles with similar injunctions regarding his identity as the Christ or Son of God (1:34; 3:12; 8:30; compare 9:9). The theme of "the messianic secret" has disputed implications for Markan Christology and may be too much for an interpreter to handle in a sermon on this single text. What is clear in this passage is that although

Jesus does not desire renown or glory for himself, the work of God being done through him will not remain a secret. Just as a tiny seed becomes a great plant (4:30-32), so Jesus' words and deeds set in motion the establishment of God's kingdom. Though it may seem strange to us, Mark's Gospel often portrays Jesus as an almost unwitting participant in this process (see 5:25-34; 7:24-29; 10:46-52). Accordingly, the emphasis in 1:42-45 is not on the leper's disobedience (for which he is neither rebuked nor punished) but on the inherent tendency of the gospel to spread. Ironically, this tendency creates inconvenience for Jesus, making his ministry increasingly difficult.

A major point, of course, is that the gospel cannot be fully understood until Jesus' ministry reaches its culmination in his death and resurrection. As Mark's story moves with some urgency toward this climactic event, a dramatic tension develops between what is already present and what is about to be. Ideally, those who benefit early from God's work in Christ will keep quiet so as not to impede the plan before it reaches fruition. But in fact what is happening cannot be hidden. The injunctions to silence have little effect, for those who experience God's salvation cannot help but speak of what they have seen and heard (compare Acts 4:20). Thus, Mark's reader is to note the overwhelming excitement of God's grace revealed in the cleansing of a leper while also realizing that this is but the beginning of the story we ought to tell. This pericope is assigned to Epiphany not Lent, but Mark's intention is for it to be recalled as a prelude to God's great salvation at the cross.

CONNECTIONS

The most obvious link between today's lessons is the healing of leprosy featured in both the first lesson and the Gospel. Early traditions about Jesus reported his ministry in terms reminiscent of the Elijah-Elisha cycle and the Gospel of Mark reports that the people of his day noted the similarities (6:15; 8:28; but see 9:11-13). Both of these lessons present healing not only as indicative of God's beneficent will for humanity, but also as an act of mercy that crosses the boundaries of politics and religion.

Scholars generally agree that the terms translated "leprosy" in English Bibles do not refer to what would be diagnosed as leprosy (Hansen's disease) through modern medicine. Rather, the words describe any number of skin disorders that mark people as ritually unclean (see Leviticus 13 and 14). Such conditions might be temporary or permanent. Sometimes, though not always, they might be contagious. Only rarely would they be debilitating, much less fatal. The greatest suffering that those so afflicted experienced was the social ostracism their condition brought upon them. The priestly codes in Israel attributed a pollution effect to what the Bible calls leprosy. Houses or fabrics that have leprosy (that is, exhibit abnormalities in their surface areas) must be destroyed (Lev. 13:47-52; 14:34-45) and affected persons must live alone, apart from human habitation (Num. 5:2-3; Lev. 13:46). Indeed, those diagnosed as lepers were required to wear torn clothes, keep their hair disheveled, cover their upper lips, and cry out "Unclean, unclean!" when approached (Lev. 13:45). The concern here is not simply contagion but defilement. Contact with lepers rendered others unclean even if they did not contract the disease. As has often been noted, the impurity attributed to lepers is essentially the same as that attributed to corpses; regardless of the severity of their disease, lepers were regarded as the "living dead" (see 2 Kings 5:7, where the ability to cure leprosy is described as power "to give life or death").

The Bible sometimes associates the leprous condition with sin, viewing it as a sign of divine displeasure or punishment. A number of people contract the condition when they are cursed by God or by God's agent: Miriam (Num. 12:10-15; Deut. 24:8-9), Joab (2 Sam. 3:29), Gehazi (2 Kings 5:25-27), Uzziah (2 Kings 15:5; 2 Chr. 26:16-21). But neither Elisha nor Jesus view the one who comes to them as being in need of repentance. Both of the stories in today's lectionary present healing as a sign of God's goodness without addressing the separate question of who does or does not meet with God's approval.

Modern preaching often makes connections between biblical leprosy and AIDS. Our present culture has tended to increase the suffering of those afflicted with AIDS by treating them as lepers—subjecting them to social ostracism, attributing their condition to moral failures, and even entertaining at times the notion that their suffering is divine punishment. Mark's emotion-charged story of Jesus touching the leper can resound with implications for a world where such attitudes persist. Notably, Mark's Gospel mentions leprosy one more time, in the brief note at 14:3 where Jesus is said to be staying at the home of Simon the leper. No healing is mentioned, but the mere fact that Jesus shares living space with a man acknowledged to be a leper implies that the prescribed social barriers are being ignored and that, accordingly, the worst effect of Simon's condition has been overcome.

The second lesson is not intentionally related to this theme but we may detect coincidental support in Paul's concern for the body. If the other two lessons tell us that God's will for the body is health, Paul emphasizes that God also wants healthy bodies to be disciplined in service to the gospel.

Seventh Sunday after the Epiphany
Seventh Sunday in Ordinary Time
Proper 2

Lectionary	First Lesson	Psalm	Second Lesson	Gospel
Revised Common	Isa. 43:18-25	Psalm 41	2 Cor. 1:18-22	Mark 2:1-12
Episcopal (BCP)	Isa. 43:18-25	Ps. 32 *or* 32:1-8	2 Cor. 1:18-22	Mark 2:1-12
Roman Catholic	Isa. 43:18-19, 21-22, 24b-25	Ps. 41:2-5, 13-14	2 Cor. 1:18-22	Mark 2:1-12
Lutheran (LBW)	Isa. 43:18-25	Psalm 41	2 Cor. 1:18-22	Mark 2:1-12

FIRST LESSON: ISAIAH 43:18-25

The first and the last verses of this lesson reverse expectations built by preceding material. In these reversals lies the gospel, the good news Second Isaiah proclaimed to the exiles during the time of the Babylonian captivity.

The surprise factor in v. 18 is lost if we do not consider the verses that come before. In 43:16-17, the prophet makes clear that the God who addresses them is indeed the Lord of the exodus, the one who "makes a way in the sea," destroying chariots and horses. We would expect the oracle to continue with an exhortation to remember this great act of deliverance in the past and to persist in the present with faith grounded in the tradition of salvation history. Instead, Isaiah says, "Do not remember the former things . . ." (v. 18). A corner has been turned. God is about to do something new (v. 19).

The new thing that God does will be like the old, but different. If God can make a way in the sea (v. 16), then God can also make a way in the desert (v. 19; NRSV, "wilderness"). The deliverance from the exile will be like an "inverse exodus." Before, God provided dry land in the midst of the waters; now, God will supply waters in the midst of the dry land (desert). In a sense, then, the new work of God recalls the old so that the tradition can never literally be forgotten but the recognition that God is going to act *now* requires dynamic faith that goes beyond commemoration of what God has done in the past. In effect, the prophet shifts the basis for hope from the historical to the eschatological. History and tradition are important, but faith looks forward, not back.

The second surprise, in v. 25, follows a traditional list of complaints God has against Israel. The people have been negligent in holding up their end of the covenant. They have not called on God, brought offerings or sacrifices, burnt incense, and so forth. Instead, they have become weary of God and burdened God with their sins and iniquities. All this prepares us for a prophetic exhortation to repentance followed by either promises or threats concerning what will happen if the exhortation is or is not heeded. But suddenly, in v. 25, God simply declares "I will not remember your sins." The forgiveness appears unmotivated, the pardon undeserved. It is grounded solely in God's self-identification as the one "who blots out your transgressions." The absolution comes for God's own sake, because of who God is, and not as a result of who the people are or of what they have done. God will keep the covenant even though God's people have not kept it. The people may have abandoned God, but God has not abandoned them.

SECOND LESSON: 2 CORINTHIANS 1:18-22

The immediate context for these verses is Paul's explanation for why he did not visit the Corinthians as they expected or as he himself had intended and announced (see 1 Cor. 16:5-7). The details of what happened are difficult to reconstruct since we are missing some of the correspondence, but the Corinthians feel that they have been slighted and that Paul's vacillation on this point can be cited as evidence that he is unreliable (1:17). In mounting his defense, Paul cannot resist digressing to reflect upon the faithfulness of God that we experience through Christ, and this digression is what occupies most of the verses chosen for today's lesson.

In contrast to "ordinary human standards" (v. 17), the faithfulness of God is certain. Paul develops this traditional concept in a specifically Christian (almost trinitarian) vein. The faithfulness of God is evident first in Jesus Christ, the Son of God who represents God's ultimate affirmation of humanity. In Jesus, Paul says, every promise of God finds fulfillment such that the perspective of God concerning humanity is always "Yes." The faithfulness of God is evident also in the Spirit, who is the guarantee of God's commitment to us. The Greek term used here (*arrabōn*) does not imply a partial payment as does the English expression "first installment" (NRSV). In modern Greek, the word is used to describe an engagement ring. The Spirit has been given in full, but this gift, complete in itself, marks only the beginning of a relationship with God that will be characterized by continued love and faithfulness.

The fact that all this is a digression is significant, indicating that Paul is more interested in proclaiming the gospel than in defending his own integrity. But the digression is not irrelevant to the matter at hand. First, God's affirmation of humanity in Christ implies also an affirmation of human relationships, including difficult ones like that between Paul and the Corinthians. Paul believes this relationship has been established by God and sealed by the Spirit (vv. 21-22) and so he persists in working with them even though they have brought each other much pain (2:1-5).

Second, and this is the point that will bring Paul back to the matter at hand, God's affirmation of us does not necessarily imply approval of all our plans. When Paul says that in Jesus "every one of God's promises is a 'Yes'" (v. 20), he does not mean that God will always give us whatever we want. God's commitment to us and to our welfare transcends the meeting of our every desire. Thus, even when God appears to say "No," this is actually subsumed under God's great "Yes" regarding who we are and what is best for us. In the same way, Paul will argue in the verses that follow that his decision not to visit Corinth was for their own benefit (possibly, to avoid precipitating a split in the congregation). Thus, his apparent "No," though disappointing, should not be taken as a diminution of his affirmation of them.

GOSPEL: MARK 2:1-12

Commentaries often give extensive treatment to this pericope because it contains the first reference to faith (as a noun) in Mark's Gospel, the first use of the term Son of Man, the first instance of conflict between Jesus and the religious leaders, and (aside from 1:4) the only mention of forgiveness of sins. The story itself is also told with vivid detail that captures the imagination and ensures a popular hearing.

The presence of faith becomes a recurrent theme in Markan miracle stories (2:5; 5:34; 10:52; compare 5:36; 6:5-6; 9:23), but no indication is ever given as to the specific content of this faith. It does not appear to be connected to any christological confession. In this passage, for instance, Mark does not say that the friends of the paralytic recognize Jesus to be the authoritative Son of Man. More likely, they exhibit faith in the word Jesus preaches (v. 2), in the message that the kingdom of God has come near (1:15). By saying that Jesus sees their faith, Mark emphasizes further that this faith is a confident trust that shows itself in action.

The link here between forgiveness of sins and healing does not necessarily imply that the man's paralysis was a divine punishment which can only be removed once his sins have been forgiven. Rather, illness and sin alike are manifestations of evil that can be overcome when God's rule is established. Likewise, the distinction between which is easier and harder (v. 9) is made with reference to verifiability rather than accomplishment. Both the forgiveness of sins and the healing of disease involve a divine abolition of evil, but the latter is easy to verify in a way that the former is not. When the paralytic rises from his bed and walks, the crowd may recognize that God has indeed removed his illness, and they may also be willing to accept Jesus' claim that God has forgiven his sins.

The charge of blasphemy (v. 7), however, implies that there is yet another dimension. If the scribes simply rejected Jesus' gospel message regarding the nearness of God's kingdom and the current availability of forgiveness, they would accuse him of heresy not blasphemy. They perceive, rightly, that Jesus intends to locate this new manifestation of divine authority in himself. The theological claim of Mark's Gospel is not simply that the rule of God has come near but that it has come near in the person and work of Jesus. If this claim were false, Jesus would indeed be a blasphemer, for he is presented here as one who professes to do what only God can do—forgive sins (2:7, 10). Ironically, as Jesus' accusers ponder this question, Mark describes Jesus as knowing their hearts, which is also something that only God can do (1 Sam. 16:7; 1 Kings 8:39; Ps. 7:9; Jer. 11:20)! Thus, Mark's readers are presented with stark alternatives regarding Jesus (true agent of God or blasphemer) but are left in no doubt as to which alternative they ought to accept.

CONNECTIONS

The obvious link between the lessons for today is their bold proclamation of the present availability of God's gracious salvation. This is a frequent theme throughout the year of the Series B lectionary with its accent on readings from Mark and John, but rarely do we see the message displayed so prominently in all three readings for a single day. This is especially true with regard to the forgiveness of sins, which is highlighted in the first lesson and the Gospel and assumed as a part of God's "Yes" in the reading from 2 Corinthians.

Early Christians proclaimed the forgiveness of sins as a present reality rather than simply a future hope (Acts 10:43). Still, as our first lesson for today reveals, long before the Christian movement took shape the prophet we know as Second Isaiah proclaimed a similar gospel. God blots out transgressions so as to remember them no more (Isa. 43:25). There is not a single verse in the New Testament that surpasses this passage as a statement of grace. Indeed, even today the implication of divine amnesia will seem extreme to many Christians. Can a God who knows the number of hairs on our heads (Matt. 10:30) ever forget anything? Yes, Isaiah insists, God can and does. God chooses to forget our sins. The skeptic will respond, "Forgive them, maybe, but not actually forget." Such incredulity rejects the image that Scripture uses advisedly and dilutes the biblical concept of forgiveness. To forgive sins, here, is to *blot them out*, to erase them, such that they never happened. In an eschatological sense, every act of forgiveness or redemption is a new creation, a reordering of life such that what went wrong is now made right. An appreciation for such an understanding of forgiveness lies behind Kierkegaard's observation that redemption is a greater miracle than creation: in the latter case God only had to make something out of nothing but in the former God had to make saints out of sinners. A failure to appreciate such an understanding of forgiveness lies behind Peter's nonsense question in Matt. 18:21 regarding how many times he ought to forgive someone: if forgiveness means to "remember no more," then anyone who is keeping count has not yet forgiven even once. In contrast to Peter, the God whom Second Isaiah envisions never has to forgive us more than once, for with a God who forgets sins, every time is always the first time.

If this seems a possible exaggeration of grace, we should look quickly at the second lesson, where Paul insists that God's word to us in Christ is *always* "Yes." We might ask whether, in contemporary society, the name of Christ is so closely associated with affirmation. More often, perhaps, the church has acquired a reputation as being the one place in our world where people are most likely to hear the word "No" spoken repeatedly. Even if we recognize appropriate reasons for this, we must lament the loss of something essential when the religion that bears Christ's name becomes known primarily as an expression of "what you must not do." In such a culture, we may perhaps fear less the dangers of preaching "cheap grace" and more the problems of proclaiming grace obscurely. Voltaire intended to mock the gospel when he wrote, "God will forgive me, for that is his business!" Deploring the flippancy, we may yet recognize that the content of this comment is not a far cry from what God says in Isa. 43:25. Paul's proclamation of the gospel also brought forth flippant responses (Rom. 6:1), but if Paul could be suspected (wrongly) of proclaiming cheap grace, he could never be suspected of proclaiming obscure grace. The latter was and still is the greater evil.

Grace does have a cost, but the cost is primarily to the giver, not the receiver. According to Isaiah, God has been burdened and wearied by sin and iniquity (43:24); according to Paul, continued affirmation of the Corinthians' interests has caused Paul "much distress, anguish of heart, and many tears" (2 Cor. 2:4). The greatest example ever of the cost of grace is introduced subtly in our reading from Mark. The forgiveness of sins comes to the paralytic as a completely free gift of grace (he was not even seeking it), but Jesus' offer of this gift costs him dearly. It brings upon him the charge of blasphemy, for which he will ultimately be put to death (Mark 14:64).

Eighth Sunday after the Epiphany
Eighth Sunday in Ordinary Time
Proper 3

Lectionary	First Lesson	Psalm	Second Lesson	Gospel
Revised Common	Hosea 2:14-20	Ps. 103:1-13, 22	2 Cor. 3:1-6	Mark 2:13-22
Episcopal (BCP)	Hosea 2:14-23	Ps. 103 or 103:1-6	2 Cor. 3:(4-11) 17—4:2	Mark 2:18-22
Roman Catholic	Hosea 2:16-17, 18, 21-22	Ps. 103:1-4, 8, 10, 12-13	2 Cor. 3:1b-6	Mark 2:18-22
Lutheran (LBW)	Hosea 2:14-16 (17-18), 19-20	Ps. 103:1-13	2 Cor. 3:1b-6	Mark 2:18-22

FIRST LESSON: HOSEA 2:14-20

The prophet Hosea was active in the Northern Kingdom of Israel during the second half of the eighth century B.C.E. This was a time of great instability, marked by religious syncretism, political assassinations (four kings in fourteen years), and the threatening rise of the Assyrian empire. It was a time of personal instability for Hosea as well, for his wife Gomer was adulterous and his marriage ended in divorce (2:2). His message to Israel is interwoven with analogies from his own life. Emotionally, the message is confused, betraying at times extreme hurt and anger and at times tender love and compassion. Hope for restoration mingles with threats of punishment but what finally comes through is that, despite Gomer's disloyalty, Hosea continues to love her, is able to forgive her, and wants her still to be his wife.

All this is the background for today's lesson expressing God's intention to allure (literally, "seduce") Israel (v. 14). According to some traditions, the wilderness was the place where Israel and Yahweh first enjoyed an idyllic relationship (Jer. 2:2-3; compare Numbers 19–24) but this "honeymoon period" came to an end with the disobedience of Achan at the Valley of Achor (Josh. 7:20-26). God's plan is to take Israel back to the honeymoon again and transform what was once an obstacle into "a door of hope" (v. 15). What is envisioned is a renewal of wedding vows, complete with a new betrothal gift—the land (vineyards) that was given before but got lost along the way. God will succeed, the prophet is sure, and the effect will be new relationships in which people are at peace with God, with nature, and with each other (vv. 16-17).

The image of God as a slighted husband and God's people as an unfaithful wife reflects a male point of view—we never hear Gomer's account of the relationship! Still, the deeply personal character of Hosea's analogy touches universal themes that transcend its gender-specific aspects. Theologically, the main point seems to be that God takes the initiative in bringing about restoration. The names of false gods will be removed from Israel's mouth (vv. 16-17) when God removes them and war will be removed from the earth when God abolishes it (v. 18). On another level, the most impressive quality of this prophet's work is its image of a God who hurts, who feels pain at our unfaithfulness and responds understandably with anger but ultimately with love.

SECOND LESSON: 2 CORINTHIANS 3:1-6

As in last week's lesson, Paul is responding to criticisms regarding his credentials. Once again he has trouble staying on the subject, evidence that he really prefers theological engagement to debate over petty issues that are significant only "according to ordinary human standards" (1:17).

This time, the issue is letters of recommendation. In the ancient world, such letters were commonplace even as they are today (see Acts 9:2; 22:5). The early church used such letters to commend recognized persons from one place to another (Acts 18:27), and Paul sometimes wrote words of commendation himself (Rom. 16:1; Phlm. 10-17). Now, some of the Corinthians want to know why Paul does not have letters commending him as do other Christians who have visited the community. Paul, of course, founded the church at Corinth. When he came to them, there was no Christian community to receive such letters nor would letters from Christian sources have made any impression on people who were not Christians. They came to believe the message of the gospel (1 Cor. 15:3-11) in "a demonstration of the Spirit and of power" (1 Cor. 2:4). Appraisals of Paul's credentials had nothing to do with their coming to faith. Paul intended it to be this way, so that their "faith might rest not on human wisdom but on the power of God" (1 Cor. 2:5).

We may surmise that now, if he wished, Paul would have no trouble collecting references from the numerous locations that have benefited from his ministry. But to do so would be to play into the hands of those who are trying to define (and evaluate) the work of God's Spirit according to ordinary human standards. Here is the great irony: throughout the world, what God has done in Corinth is proclaimed among Christians as a testimony to the work of the Spirit. The Corinthians are themselves a letter of recommendation, a testimony primarily to Christ, but also in a secondary sense to Paul and his companions through whom this great work of the Spirit was prepared. If others can read this living testimony in the hearts of the

Corinthian people, then why do the Corinthians themselves think they need some official certification to authenticate what God has done for them? We should not exaggerate Paul's response here in a way that makes him the prototype of freewheeling charismatics who answer only to God and have no respect for ecclesiastical order. Letters of reference have their place, but it is the Spirit who gives life (v. 6) and something has gone wrong with a church that cannot recognize the Spirit at work.

With all this talk about letters and the Spirit, Paul cannot help but drift into another matter closer to his heart: the contrast between the letter of the law and the spirit of the gospel. This discussion, which is developed at more length in Romans (see 7:6) is alluded to here in mention of "tablets of stone" (v. 3) and "a new covenant" (v. 6). Indeed, it is assumed in the final declaration that "the letter kills, but the Spirit gives life," which makes little sense otherwise (letters of recommendation do not kill). Paul is not opposed to the written law as such—it derives from God and reflects divine will. But for Paul, the written law has brought people to experience the condemnation of God. The new covenant (Jer. 31:31; 1 Cor. 11:25) of the gospel brings confidence through Christ toward God (v. 4).

GOSPEL: MARK 2:13-22

A tension between old and new runs throughout Mark's Gospel and arises especially in lessons appointed for the Epiphany season. Jesus brings "a new teaching" (1:27), which Mark also describes as "the gospel of God" (1:14). This gospel consists of the message that "the kingdom of God has come near" in the person and work of Jesus (1:15). Jesus proclaims this message through word and deed, by teaching and preaching (1:21-22, 38-39; 2:2, 13) and by healing (1:31, 34, 41; 2:11), casting out demons (1:25, 34, 39), and authoritatively forgiving sins (2:5). But, as the pivotal section in Mark 2:1—3:6 demonstrates, the gospel Jesus proclaims creates havoc with traditional conceptions of religion.

The centerpiece to this section is the last two verses of today's lesson. On the surface, the metaphors of unshrunk cloth and new wine are easy to understand. The new teaching of Jesus is incompatible with the old ways. Jesus does not intend simply to patch up the holes where traditional religion has failed or to provide the traditional religious system with new content. The gospel of God's rule is more radical than that. It cannot be simply appended to traditional religion or contained by any religious system. Mark 2:1-3:6 offers stories that illustrate how this is so.

In the story of the paralytic considered last week (2:1-12), Jesus strikes to the very heart of religion by declaring that a person's sins are simply forgiven. The declaration has no apparent motivation—the paralytic did not perform any sacrifices or participate in any prescribed rituals. He did not exhibit any signs of remorse or repentance. In fact, he did not even confess his sins or request forgiveness. If God chooses to forgive people as casually as this, then religion—all religion, not just Judaism—is in trouble.

In case people do not get the point, Jesus acts out the implications of this gospel by calling a despised (and probably despicable) tax collector to join his community. Then, he openly eats with this person and "many tax collectors and sinners" (v. 15) in an act of fellowship that demonstrates his acceptance of them and solidarity with them. We must not tone down this passage by suggesting such people were "sinners" primarily in the eyes of the Pharisees, perhaps because they broke purity codes through their contact with Gentiles or the like. Recent scholarship has shown that tax collectors were universally despised in the ancient world primarily because corruption within the system itself invited and perhaps necessitated rampant dishonesty and oppressive measures. Besides, Mark 2:15 and 17 indicate that Jesus' table partners are sinners in the eyes of the evangelist and Jesus also. They are not just victims of a self-righteous, legalistic system. They are bad people. Furthermore, nothing in the text indicates that these are ex-sinners or penitents who are now determined to mend their ways. The point of Jesus' acted parable is to leave no doubt as to what the implications of a gospel of unmerited forgiveness must be. The radical inclusiveness of such a gospel is unlikely to fit comfortably into any known religious system then or now.

Ultimately, however, the matter becomes more complex. The metaphors of the cloth and wine express concern that the old not be destroyed. In the story that immediately precedes these sayings (2:18-20) Jesus does not say that fasting is part of the old system that no longer has any place. Instead, he insists that it will continue to have a place in the lives of his followers (v. 20). True, the dawn of God's kingdom signals a new era of joy like that of a wedding banquet and fasting at such a time seems inappropriate. But the reference to a time "when the bridegroom is taken away" serves as a reminder that, though the kingdom has "come near" (1:15), it has not yet arrived in its fullness. Until it does, religious observances such as fasting will continue to have their place. Thus the tension between new and old, between the gospel and religion, is grounded in the eschatological tension between the "already" and the "not yet." The new life of the gospel is lived in celebration of the former, in anticipation of the latter, and in recognition of the difference.

CONNECTIONS

The tension between new and old sounded so clearly in our Gospel lesson (Mark 2:21-22) echoes through the other two lessons for today also. In Hosea, as in the first part of the Gospel lesson (Mark 2:13-17), the emphasis is on restoration of a relationship between God and those who have become alienated from God. The restoration may be a new thing, but it actually consists of recovering what is old, of regaining the life that was lost or discovering what life was always intended to be. Both texts present the restoration as being initiated and accomplished through divine activity. Inducement to repentance is not primary in either text, but rather affirmation that mercy will prevail. God's tenderness will win Israel over and Jesus' fellowship will have a healing effect (Mark 2:17).

The second lesson picks up on the tension between new and old evident in the latter part of our Gospel reading (Mark 2:18-20). Letters of reference and ritual fasting may both be good things but those who are preoccupied with rules for such matters run the risk of missing out on the celebration of life in the Spirit. The church must always seek to discern what is essential from what is *adiaphora* (nonessential, though not necessarily unimportant).

The Transfiguration of Our Lord
Last Sunday of the Epiphany

Lectionary	First Lesson	Psalm	Second Lesson	Gospel
Revised Common	2 Kings 2:1-12	Ps. 50:1-6	2 Cor. 4:3-6	Mark 9:2-9
Episcopal (BCP)	1 Kings 19:9-18	Ps. 27 or 27:5-11	2 Pet. 1:16-19 (20-21)	Mark 9:2-9
Roman Catholic	Dan. 7:9-10, 13-14	Ps. 97:1-2, 5-6, 9	2 Pet. 1:16-19	Mark 9:2-10
Lutheran (LBW)	2 Kings 2:1-12a	Ps. 50:1-6	2 Cor. 3:12—4:2	Mark 9:2-9

FIRST LESSON: 2 KINGS 2:1-12

With the possible exception of Enoch (Gen. 5:24), Elijah is the only character in biblical narrative to be taken directly to heaven without experiencing death. He ascends in a whirlwind (vv. 1, 11) accompanied by angels in fiery chariots, though careless interpreters soon placed him in a chariot himself (see Sir. 48:9) and that is where he has been in religious art and popular imagination ever since. Because Elijah was spared death, prophetic tradition held that he would someday return (Mal. 4:5-6), which is why an empty chair is often reserved for him at Jewish Passover meals. Christian interpreters spiritualized this tradition in two different directions. The Gospel of Matthew reflects the notion that the coming of John the Baptist fulfilled the prophecy of Elijah's return (Matt. 17:10-13). The Lukan tradition prefers to regard Jesus himself as fulfilling this role. The latter idea is especially prominent in Luke's story of Jesus' ascension (Acts 1:6-11), which is closely connected to our lesson for today (much more so than Mark's account of the Transfiguration!).

One motif in today's lesson concerns Elisha's desire to remain with his master as long as possible (vv. 2, 4) and his great sorrow at their inevitable parting (v. 12). His knowledge and acceptance of this transition as the will of God (vv. 3, 5) may make it bearable, but it does not make it easy. The story is told with deliberate emotion, for biblical writers tended to be less embarrassed by sentiment than modern theologians.

Elisha had already been designated the successor of Elijah when the latter cast his mantle upon him (1 Kings 19:19-21). Now that succession is confirmed and fulfilled through the bestowal of a double share of Elijah's spirit on his disciple. The latter expression does not mean that Elisha has twice the spirit or power of Elijah, but that he inherits twice as much of Elijah's spirit as anyone else, marking him as the "eldest son" (Deut. 21:17) and leader of the community of followers. The condition Elijah lays down for this transfer (v. 10) confirms that it is not his but God's to grant (compare Mark 10:40). If God grants Elisha to see into the heavenly realm, then the young prophet will know he has received what he desired. This happens, and so Elisha is justified to call his master, "Father" (v. 12).

The main point of the story is that God does not leave people without prophetic and spiritual leadership (compare the first lesson for the Second Sunday after the Epiphany). When Elijah parts the waters of the Jordan in v. 8, he shows that he is a true successor to Joshua (Joshua 3), who in turn was successor to Moses (Exod. 14:21-22). After Elijah is gone, Elisha too will part these waters as a sign that "the Lord the God of Elijah" is with him also (2 Kings 2:13-14). Devotion to human leaders is commendable, but ultimately God is the one who cares for us, raising up new leaders when the ones we trust are gone.

SECOND LESSON: 2 CORINTHIANS 4:3-6

A few verses back (2 Cor. 3:7), Paul seized on the image of Moses veiling his face at Sinai (see Exod. 34:29-35) to make a point about the transience of the old covenant of the law. From there, he went on to say that even now the minds of some are veiled so that apart from the Lord's help the revelation of Christ in the Scriptures cannot be seen (2 Cor. 3:14-16). Continuing in this same vein, Paul now contrasts the work of "the god of this world" (the devil) with that of the creator God. The former blinds the minds of people to the glory of Christ while the latter shines light into our hearts to give knowledge of Christ's glory, which is indeed the glory of God.

Paul is not here developing a doctrine of predestination, nor does he intend to offer an adequate explanation for why God should reveal the truth to some but not all. Rather, he wants to define our context for ministry. The task is to "proclaim Jesus Christ as Lord" (v. 5), but when we do so, we must realize that forces far greater than ourselves oppose us. Thus, we should not be surprised when the good news we announce is rejected. Even when it is accepted we should recognize this as the miraculous work of God overcoming the powerful resistance. This is why ministers of the gospel must remain "slaves for Jesus' sake" (v. 5) who do not proclaim themselves.

This text is also valued for its christological proclamation. Jesus is described here as "the image of God" (v. 4) and as the one in whose face the glory of God becomes recognizable (v. 6). Such passages are least meaningful when taken as proof texts for the divinity of Christ, which is not the issue here. Paul's concern, as C. K. Barrett has observed in his volume *The Second Epistle to the Corinthians* (New York: Harper & Row, 1973), is that we come to apprehend the divinity *of God* (p. 132). In other words, the glory of Christ that is revealed in the gospel (v. 4) enlightens us to know what it means for God to be God. The reference to Gen. 1:3, furthermore, implies that God's revelation in Christ is comparable to a new creation (2 Cor. 5:17). Coming to know God through Christ is tantamount to having the initial act of creation repeated in our hearts.

GOSPEL: MARK 9:2-9

Previews of coming attractions have become ubiquitous in modern cinema to the extent that we now see them not only at the theater but also on television and rented videotapes. In this pericope, Mark's Gospel offers a preview of the glory that Jesus and his disciples will eventually share when the kingdom of God has come in its fullness. Jesus has just said, "there are some standing here who will not taste death until they see that the kingdom of God has come with power" (9:1). For three of his disciples, the promise is now fulfilled. Jesus' very appearance is altered, his clothes becoming dazzling white. Moses and Elijah suddenly appear with him, a cloud overshadows the whole group, and from out of the cloud God announces that Jesus is "my Son, the Beloved!" This is the second of three great proclamations of Jesus as the divine Son in Mark. The first is made by God to Jesus alone (1:9-11), this one is made by God to humans, and the third will be made by a human at the foot of the cross (15:39).

Commentaries have a field day with the details of this passage, especially with regard to the significance of Moses and Elijah (or, to be precise, "Elijah with Moses," v. 4). Why these two representatives of Israel's past? Together, they may represent the law and the prophets (though Moses alone could do that, being known as preeminent prophet as well as lawgiver). They are both figures who have experienced theophanies on mountains (Moses: Exod. 24:15-18; Elijah: 1 Kings 19:9-12). Both are eschatological figures, whose return was in some sense expected during the end time (a prophet *like* Moses in Deut. 18:18; Elijah himself in Mal. 4:5-6). All these points may contribute in some way to the imagery but Mark does not capitalize on any of them. Likewise, the "six days" mentioned in v. 2 could be a recollection of the six days of preparation for Moses' experience (Exod. 24:16), and such features as physical transformation, the presence of light, and the voice from the cloud are reminiscent of Moses' experience on Sinai. But these are common elements in theophanies and the divine preference for occurrence of events on a seventh day is well established.

Focus on the details may cause us to miss the big picture. The appearance of a glorified Jesus on a mountain (near heaven) talking with prominent figures from Israel's past is a glimpse into the heavenly realm, the realm beyond death, beyond what we usually conceive of as space and time. Why Elijah and Moses instead of, say, Isaiah or Abraham or David? We may as well ask why Jesus elsewhere refers to life in the glorious kingdom of heaven as eating "with Abraham, Isaac, and Jacob" (Matt. 8:11). The other Gospels, perhaps, make more of the Moses and Elijah typologies, to the extent that Luke considers the topic of conversation at the Transfiguration to be important (Jesus' departure or, literally, *exodus*, Luke 9:31). But in Mark, the glorified presence of Jesus in fellowship with heavenly figures is a captivating image that stands on its own.

This glimpse into the future, this foretaste of heavenly glory comes right after Jesus' first prediction of his passion (Mark 8:31-38). The purpose of the preview is to let the disciples know where the way of the cross eventually leads. Jesus' disciples are called to deny themselves, to bear their crosses, and to lose their lives for the sake of Jesus and the gospel (8:34-35). But suffering and service is not final. It is not the ultimate human experience. Jesus has also spoken of a time when he will come in his glory (8:38; compare 14:62) and now he shows the inner circle of his followers just what this will mean. Glorious transformation in a world beyond death is not some idealistic dream or naive hope; it is a reality that in this story enters proleptically into human history for a few moments in a way that can actually be seen and experienced.

Ironically, but not surprisingly, the selected disciples do not seem to get the point. Peter, understandably frightened, does "not know what to say" but this does not prevent him from saying it anyway (vv. 5-6). Numerous sermons have built on Peter's desire to prolong the glorious mountaintop experience while ignoring the need for ministry that still remains in the valley below (Mark 9:14-18). This is true, but there is more. Peter's pointless verbosity reveals that he is as uncomfortable on the mountaintop as he would be elsewhere. All he is called to do at the Transfiguration is to be there, but like many people in our Western culture, Peter is more comfortable with *doing* than *being*. He is at this point as unable to worship on the mountain as he is unfit for service in the valley.

Peter's offer to build booths may also reflect a grave misunderstanding that mistakes the preview of glory for the final consummation itself. Apocalyptic tradition held that at the end time God would "tabernacle" with God's people and dwell with them as in the days of old (Zech. 14:16-19; compare Exod. 33:7-11). But to want glory immediately and ignore what Jesus has said about suffering and service in the meantime represents only one way to miss the point of the preview. A second, ultimately more serious way to miss out will be to forget the glory that awaits altogether and surrender to despair when the costs of discipleship become too great. This, of course, is precisely what happens to Peter and the others in the passion story (14:50, 66-72). Mark offers us the story of the Transfiguration, along with the negative examples of the original disciples, in order that we might listen to the Son of God in a way that they did not (v. 7) and hear what he says about both suffering and glory.

CONNECTIONS

In the Gospel of Mark the story of the Transfiguration serves as a transition between an account of Jesus' Galilean ministry, which is marked by wondrous miracles, and an account of his journey to Jerusalem, which is marked by suffering and death. Similarly, in the church year, the day of Transfiguration marks a transition between the season of Epiphany that celebrates the glorious revelation of God in Christ and the more somber observances of Lent that begin with Ash Wednesday just three days later.

All three of the lessons for this day emphasize the glory of God and present this glory as something that can be experienced in extraordinary ways here and now. While some churches may exult in such texts, many Christian leaders approach them soberly, concerned about the triumphalism and misplaced orientation toward success that a theology of glory can engender. In this age of cynicism, however, too much caution in this regard may not be the right approach. For every one parishioner who "is too heavenly minded to be of any earthly good," we may have several whose religion is so down-to-earth that it lacks transcendence. Faith obviously needs to deal with real life but it ought also to provide vision that takes us beyond the mundane or harsh qualities of daily living.

The second lesson for today is the ultimate Epiphany text: "God has shone in our hearts to give the light." Glory is not something to be achieved through human effort but is a manifestation of God given to us. This is important to remember when interpreting Mark's Gospel, which might otherwise be read as implying that disciples achieve glory *through* suffering and service. Not so. Service to the point of suffering is called for now, and glory is promised for the future, but the two are not connected as means to end. Jesus reveals that God intends a glorious future for us. This is our destiny. Even if we fail at service, as do Jesus' disciples, we are still "bound for glory." We ought to serve others, then, not in order to achieve the glory (which is promised us in any case) but, simply, because this is the right thing to do. It is what God expects.

Both the first lesson and the Gospel offer glimpses of the future, of the life with God that lies beyond this world. The second lesson speaks in the past tense (God *has shone*), in reference probably to the resurrection, the moment when new light burst forth in the cosmos that destroys the darkness of death and penetrates our very hearts. At this point in the church year we look forward to the celebration of that great event at Easter, and at this and every point in history we look forward to the consummation of what God has thus begun at the parousia. As preachers, we must not underestimate the power of anticipation. The story of the Transfiguration is one of the biblical texts that may have inspired Martin Luther King in his famous " I Have a Dream" sermon. Having "been to the mountaintop," he had obtained a vision of life as God intends. Ultimately, these visions of the future do not take us out of this world, but enable us to view the present in light of what is to be.